Famous Shipwrecks of the Florida Keys

Volume I

Robert "Frogfoot" Weller

EBSCO Media, Birmingham, AL 35233
1990

ISBN 0-9628359-0-0

Library of Congress Catalog-in-Publication data:

Weller, Robert M.
Famous Shipwrecks of the Florida Keys V-1

Cover: "Storm Beset," Original painting by Eldred Clark Johnson

Robert "Frogfoot" Weller

The author has always been a water-baby, born and raised along the Detroit River in Wyandotte, Michigan. During WWII he joined the Navy V-12 program, attending Williams College in Massachusetts, then midshipman's school at Fort Schuyler, N.Y. where he received a commission. The end of the war found him floating from island to island in the Pacific aboard a refrigerator ship. During the Korean War he was a frogman with UDT-1, and was aptly nicknamed "Frogfoot." Finally released to civilian life in 1954 he went back to the educational system, graduating from the University of Delaware as a civil engineer in 1957. Joining Honeywell he worked first in North Carolina, then headed south to Florida where he has permanently dropped his anchor. In 1982 he retired from the Milton Roy Co. and started his own cabinet business, one that pays the bills while the Wellers are off treasure diving.

Other books by Robert "Frogfoot" Weller
Sunken Treasure on Florida Reefs, 1987

Margaret Weller

Born in the tropical setting of Trinidad with the enchanting background of steel drums and a gentle Caribbean breeze, Margaret has always been a water flower. At the time, her father, a ruddy Englishman, worked for Shell Oil and it wasn't unusual for the Mathews family to spend much of their traveling time on the more glamorous ships like the *Queen Mary*, en route to far-away places that *National Geographic* readers only dream about.

After a try at college life in Georiga and Florida, Margaret married and lived for a while in Venezuela where her sons Alan and Robbie were born. As some marriages have a habit of not quite working out, she moved to Florida with her two boys and again took up housekeeping with her parents who had retired there. While working as a tour guide and business manager of the Miami Serpentarium, the Weller side of her life developed. Bob "Frogfoot" Weller always had an uncanny eye for beauty—and here was one surrounded by reptiles and in need of saving! This handsome devil swooped her off her feet with tales of sunken treasure and riches beyond imagination. They were married in 1974, and have for the past 16 years been romantically following the trail of "Pieces of Eight" and "Gold Doubloons." Margaret is the binder that holds their treasure diving operation "Crossed Anchors Salvage" together. When days, weeks, even months of frustration at finding absolutely nothing begins to wear down on the divers, Margaret's easy laugh and a "Tomorrow we'll find it" smile is enough to keep spirits high. And the treasure is there! Bob and Margaret together have recovered enough gold, silver, jewelry and artifacts to fill a museum. Margaret and Deo Fisher are the only woman divers to ever recover a "Royal," a perfect gold coin struck as a presentation piece for the King of Spain. She's one in a million.

With blood, sweat, money and technology the diver works a treasure site until frustration and endurance become inseparable. Almost as the decision is made to toss it all, the sea gives up some of its treasure, and you're hooked!

Bob "Frogfoot" Weller 1980

Table of Contents

FOREWORD

There is an aura of mystery around treasure salvage. Read in newsprint, viewed on television, the principal players seem to lead a life of excitement and mystique around which rumors flourish and feed. In today's society young people do not have much to dream about, but as long as there are gold Doubloons and silver Pieces of Eight on the bottom of the ocean . . . their dreams can still come true. Whatever the case, it has always been inspirational, and certainly sunken treasure is what dreams are made of.

When I made my move to Miami in 1960 it was with that objective. As a Frogman in Korea I had a close personal relationship with the underwater world. On the bottom of the ocean I felt as comfortable as sitting in my own living room. After two wars, and all the education I felt I would ever need, I decided to live in a part of the States where I could enjoy my leisure time 12 months out of every year. I was willing to work standing on my head if I had to, as long as the weekends belonged to me. I loved the water, and after Korea the warm, clear waters of Florida became the objective. It was my reasons for hard work and the educational grind it took to get there.

Diving shipwrecks off the coast of Delaware during the summers of 1954-57 helped get me through the rigors of structural mechanics and the theory of equations at the University of Delaware. The Delaware Underwater Swim Club was great therapy for my family as well as myself. My sons Robert and Richard were at an age where weekends on the beach and on the dive boats brought us the few moments together in a schedule that found me at the University eight hours a day, and working as a janitor till midnight. It also gave me my first taste of wreck-diving, one that soon supplanted spearing fish and underwater photography. The wrecks off the coast of Delaware were primarily modern, with the exception of the *Faithful Steward*. Here was a wreck that was close to the beach, supplying copper coins dated 1774-1782 to beach-combers after every nor'easter. My first trip to "Coin Road" three miles south of Rehobeth, De. was a memorable one. Doug Haven, a DuPont engineer, and I played hookie the day the wind howled out of the northeast and the beach began to cut away. A call from John Marsh in Rehobeth that there should be coins on the beach sent us speeding the 105 miles along Route 13 to the ocean. That day the tide was high and waves were just breaking over the six foot dune line that keeps the ocean from wiping out traffic along the ocean highway. As we parked the car and climbed the sand dune, a wave deposited a copper English penny at my feet. I could hardly believe that it would be that easy finding treasure. This coin was plainly dated 1776, the year of the Revolution, and it had been tumbled by the sand to a bright copper finish. That day as Doug and I scoured the 5 foot cut into the dune line we picked up 50 copper coins, both English and Irish, as well as several keys and an old lock. It was my first real treasure, and it was exciting.

To me it was like opening a door and turning the lights on. Suddenly here was something I could get very excited about. The weeks and months that followed found me digging through old records and newspaper articles on this ship that apparently lay so near the beach. It carried 350,000 copper coins, enough to help relieve the lack of hard currency in the new independent United States. As the story of the *Faithful Steward* unfolded, it was also clear that a great many ships had sunk along not only the coast of Delaware, but the entire eastern seaboard. Not all of them carried treasure, but history in the form of artifacts is as much a treasure as gold and silver. A professor at the University, Arthur Jarvela, one day passed along the information that silver "Pieces of Eight" were being picked up after a storm at the very south end of Long Beach, on the coast of New Jersey. By that time the collection of copper coins had grown substantially, so the fires of my enthusiasm for a Piece of Eight found me driving weekends the 85 miles to the coast of New Jersey. South of Beach Haven the spit of land was desolate, and without a northeaster the silver lay buried under 5-6 feet of sand. I stood alone one day on this narrow stretch of beach with the realization that not too far offshore there lay a Spanish Galleon with what I considered "treasure" on board. The water was murky, cold and uninviting. But the fire inside of me shouted "Go for it!" Some kind of a decision must have been made that day, because the choice of avocation upon graduation was clear after that. My objective, Florida and the shipwreck sites of old Spanish Galleons.

As far as I knew there was only one place on the eastern seaboard where you could find the trail of galleons and their treasure. It was along the Florida Keys and up the coast as far as Cape Canaveral. Here the galleons had to tack back and forth in the narrow waist of the Bahama Channel, each time coming close enough to take visual bearings on the Florida coastline before tacking back towards the Bahama Banks. The dragons teeth of the Florida reefs extend seaward from several hundred yards to as much as five miles, a natural hazard for these frail freight trains of the sea. But their greatest peril lie in the unpredictable hurricanes that seemed to spring from nowhere, and so suddenly there was no turning back. Of the billions of dollars in gold and silver that was carried back to Spain from the New World mines, for the most part it had to travel this route, and an estimated 10 percent was lost to pirates and shipwrecks caused by poor navigation or hurricanes. At least two major fleets of Spanish treasure galleons, the 1715 and the 1733 fleets, were almost completely destroyed by hurricanes in the Bahama Channel.

After graduation in 1957 I accepted a position with Honeywell in the Tampa, Florida office. Our son Patrick was born shortly afterwards and for the Weller family all the hard work and long hours seemed to have paid off. But it was short-lived. Honeywell moved us to North Carolina for what was promised a short "tour of duty," but stretched into three years of top sales performance before an opening in the Miami office started our final caravan southward.

When I arrived in Miami in 1960 the salvage of the 1733 Spanish fleet of 18 wreck-sites had just begun. Tim Watkins and his crew on the *Buccaneer* had partially salvaged the *El Infante* on Little Conch Reef in 1957, and Art McKee had already worked several years on the *Capitana* of the fleet the *El Rubi* off Tavernier Island. It seemed every week the *Miami Herald* had new stories of sunken treasure being recovered from the Keys. From our home in South Miami I had an open road into the keys. In 1960 all that was needed was a small trailerable boat, a reliable outboard engine, and an air-lift. Highway US #1 into the Keys was narrow, the bridges were a tight squeeze if you met a Greyhound bus coming in the opposite direction, but overall the traffic was manageable. There were several salvage diving groups that were actively pursuing the virgin ballast piles, and as each wreck-site was located and salvaged the excitement was as thick as mosquitos in the mangroves. Artifacts that were recovered could be seen in bank exhibits and local museum displays. There was a mutual understanding within the salvage groups that transcended all legal lines. It was simple. The divers that first located a wreck-site worked them without interference from the other groups, an understanding of mutual respect that everyone was willing to abide by. Those early years were some of the greatest salvage years ever experienced in the Florida Keys. It took some interpretation of the early 1733 Spanish maps, and there were at least three of them, to determine the most logical place to search. The maps were crude and many of today's smaller islands in the Keys are man-made to provide the roadbed for bridges now spanning the Keys. Shapes of the larger islands looked different to the Spanish than they do today to the surveyors with aerial assistance.

It was difficult to judge distances on these earlier Spanish charts until it was determined that the 1733 salvage camp was located on the north end of Islamorada. Here fresh water was available, but the "flies caused great miseries." On the charts the reefs near the salvage camp were more clearly plotted so that salvage vessels could find their way into the area now known as Whale Harbor without grounding. With this information it was a natural assumption that the distances between nearby Rodriquez Island, Tavernier Island, and Dove Key would be as accurate as any distances measured by the Spanish. Taking an old pair of navigator dividers recovered from one of the shipwrecks, we carefully measured the distances from these known landmarks, and with this as a guide began stepping off distances along the old Spanish chart. It soon became clear where the Spanish perceived the various major Florida Keys to be. The reefs and shipwreck locations then became a race for the divers with the time and ability to read the reefs and visualize the 1733 disaster. The salvage divers of the 60's started what must be known in future and historical biographies as "The treasure salvage years." They made it happen, gave realism to everyone's dream of sunken treasure. It is to these divers I dedicate this book.

The author's salvage boat "Pandion" docked behind the Smith's residence, lower Matecumbe Key, FL.

Acknowledgments

There are a number of salvage divers that have helped me re-create the early years when we salvaged the ballast mounds along the Florida Keys. Before memories fade I want to credit captain Bobby Klein, a great diver and invaluable asset to many of the 1733 sites and *HMS Winchester.* Jack Haskins has always been a source of good background information as well as one of the best salvage divers in the business. His knowledge and readability of the old Spanish *legajos* has added the spice to many of these stories. Richard MacAllaster is a salvage diver first class. Richard has never tried to put icing on the cake, he only tells it the way it is. His adaptation of Richard Gilmore's triangulation grid has advanced site salvage procedures immeasurably. Helping MacAllaster and Haskins salvage the *Angustias* put a few building blocks in my salvage career. Craig Hamilton introduced me to the *El Infante* in 1960, and inspired in me the hope some day I would find my own "1732 Pillar Dollar." John Berrier, a retired Navy officer like myself, has fulfilled the treasure dream we all must have. At one sitting he can weave a dream of salvage that will convince anyone to head for the reefs. Art Sapp and Bobby Savage were familiar faces on every site, and always good for a hot cup of coffee. Tim Watkins, and his *Buccaneer* crew Olin Frick, Jim Green, Jim Hittell, Paul Nixon, and Jim Doyle, were responsible for the first "Treasure War" and very much in the headlines during those early years. Doc Welberry, the Roberts brothers, and Marty Meylach were instrumental in keeping treasure fever at a high with their individual recoveries. And no one can forget Don Gurgiolo and his oil-leaking SeaBee amphibious airplane. In spite of its aerodynamic quirks it helped locate several ballast piles.

Bobby Jordan has been treasure diving in the Florida Keys most of his life. With Mel Fisher's "Armada Research" he worked the Coffin Patch site of the *San Ignacio,* and later made headline news when he located the *Santa Margarita,* sister ship of the *Atocha.* Art Hartman has been active on both sides of the Bahama Banks and has developed one of the better magnetometers. His recent recoveries on *las Maravillas* are world famous. John and Judy Halas are the benchmarks in Key Largo. When John metal detects the bottom his cohorts agree he "leaves nothing." Judy has helped make some great recoveries on the 1715 fleet, and has put the experience to great use in fostering a column for the *Miami Herald.* Duke Long, Carl Fismer, Henry Taylor, Jim King, Chuck Mitchell, are all well known for their salvage activities in the Keys. No treasure book would be complete without its own Tom Gurr. Tom battled all odds great and small, lost—then dumped his treasure back in the ocean. He made the *San Jose* story come to life, as painful as it was, to be shared by all of us.

Undoubtedly there are many divers that worked the Keys in those early days that I have left out, and to those I've forgotten—I apologize; we'll make up for it in the next volume.

Above water a lot of work went into putting this book together. My wife heads up the list in support and encouragement to "capture the moments of glory" when treasure history was being written. As a diver she has been on the bottom with us when some the greatest recoveries have been made. Ernie Richards, photographer extraordinary, provides this book with most of the photos. With a bottle of Dramamine in one hand and a camera in the other the site photos became possible. A salvage diver as well, he knows how impossible it is to locate wreck-sites without good bearings. He did a great job. A salvage diver, Duke Long is a world renowned artist as well. His sketches of the various wreck-sites makes them easier to locate and enjoy. Bernie and Marge Smith's home away from home in the Florida Keys provided the jumping off point as I re-visited the old wreck-sites to do the Loran co-ordinates and photography. Bernie, Kip Porter, and I spent time on the *San Jose,* the *El Infante,* and *San Pedro.* We share some great stories concerning the raising of cannon, and just having "fun" diving weekends on the countless number of wreck-sites that line the Florida reefs. Finally, Jim Miller and Roger Smith, State of Florida Bureau of Records and Management, made available the microfilm of *legajos* from the Spanish archives. Dr. Alan Craig, of FAU, translated the old Spanish and helped decipher the more difficult passages. With this information a more comprehensive picture of the 1733 disaster became possible.

Visiting the wreck-sites.

Many of the sites are several miles off-shore, and although telephoto lenses were used, it became necessary to close on many of the landmarks in order to get definition on what was being photographed. So do not be fooled if the land mass appears much closer than it actually is in the photos. The *San Jose* is presently under lease to Dr. Ron Molinari of Tavernier. You may visit the site but please keep clear of the salvage boats that may be in the area. The *Winchester* is in Pennecamp State Park. The reef is outstanding and will provide some great photo opportunities, but nothing can be removed from the site. The *Alligator* is one of the easiest wrecks to visit and the water is fairly shallow and crystal clear. Great for family diving and photography. Duncan Mathewson presently runs archeology instruction tours to this site. The *Populo* also is in Pennecamp Park, and although well marked by the reef it lies against, may be difficult to locate if the surface is choppy and the skies overcast. Use Loran co-ordinates to get in the area then look for the reef. The *Angustias* and *Sueco* are easily located and fun to dive. Be careful of the current running under Long Key bridge on the *Angustias,* and as a precaution tether an inner tube or life preserver some distance astern of your boat. You will enjoy every dive, and hopefully treasure the moment you dove one of the "Famous Shipwrecks of the Florida Keys."

Bernie and Marge Smith provided the winter home for the Pandion crew.

Chapter I
El Populo 1733

Alias: El Pingue, Nuestra
    Señora del Populo
Loran: 14177.7, 62191.2
Latitude: 25° 21.3'
Longitude: 80° 10.0'

Captain Imbernon must have felt jinxed. His ship *El Populo* had survived the first onslaught of the hurricane. After being driven into shallow water he dropped his anchor inside the dragons teeth that rimmed the Florida Keys, letting out the full scope of his anchor to get a good grip on the sandy bottom. The seas still mounted 20' waves, but for the time being he was holding his own. Then — the eye of the hurricane passed, the wind shifted rapidly and now blew from the opposite direction. The *Populo* swung on the arc of the anchor line, striking first one coral head that ruptured her bottom. Then as it spilled ballast across the sandy bottom it began to fill with water, striking hard against another reef 200 yards to the east. Here the *Populo* settled to the bottom in 32 feet of water, at the base of the reef that became her resting place.

The Populo was a *Guerra* or war scout ship belonging to the King of Spain. Because Captain Imbernon's ship was a fast corvette type, and not too large, it stayed near the van of the 21 ships that comprised the Spanish 1733 Silver Plate Fleet. When the hurricane struck from the southeast the *Populo* was driven through the reefs near the north end of Key Largo. Now she lay alongside the reef with water up to her poop deck, and her primary cargo of tobacco was a soggy bulge in her lower hold. The ship's longboat was still intact, and Imbernon could see the fleet *Aviso Delores* lying at a rakish angle on a reef nearby. The *Aviso's* longboat was also intact, and together the two crews rowed to a nearby island where they learned from the local Indians that "Many masts were above the water to the south." Captain Huboni on the *El Africa* had been at the van of the fleet as it sailed up the Bahama Channel. When the hurricane struck he was able to keep his ship clear of the reefs, and anchored in 40 *brazos* (200') of water. After the storm passed he began a survey of the damage to the Spanish fleet, and just inside the reefs at the head of the *Martires*, he sighted the *aviso*. The ship was still intact, but grounded on a reef. He sent his longboat to see if he could rescue the crew and salvage its cargo. As the longboat drew near the crew sighted the *Populo* with its decks awash against a reef nearby. No one was found on board either ship, but some movement was observed on shore. As the longboat threaded its way through the reefs toward shore they discovered the other longboats, and the crews of both vessels. Everyone was in great spirits to find so many survivors, and to be rescued. With everyone safely on board his ship, Captain Huboni sailed southward to view the carnage of his sister ships as they lay scattered over the reefs. He was able to rescue many other survivors before sailing back to Havana to report the loss of the fleet. In the following months salvage efforts were successful in refloating the *aviso*, and she was used to help recover treasure from the wreck-sites along the Matecumbes. The *Populo* was a total loss, and slipped into the archives of oblivion.

By the fall of 1966, after 6 active years of searching by professional salvage groups, 10 of the 1733 Spanish Silver Plate Fleet shipwrecks had been located. Press and TV coverage made headline news as the *El Infante, Capitana, Herrerra, Tres Puentes, San Pedro, El Terri, Almiranta, Chavez, Sueco,* and *San Fernando* gave up their treasures. During the Spanish salvage operations in 1733 at least three of the ships, the *Murgia, Gran Poder,* and *aviso,* were refloated and sailed back to Spain. A fourth ship the *El Africa* had managed to stay clear of the reefs during the hurricane and carried survivors back to Havana. Of the remaining seven wreck-sites only two were thought to have sunk outside the three mile limit. The *Populo* lay somewhere near Pacific Reef Light, and the *San Jose* off Tavernier Island. The records and charts of the Spanish were fairly accurate, but still it was a big ocean. Beyond the three mile limit, and nearly out of sight of land, there were few landmarks to guide the hunt. The reefs are the best roadmaps, but when wrapped in a blanket of murky visibility, even these are not much help. Working outside the three mile limit had its advantages. By 1966 the State of Florida's grip on salvage had tightened. Inside the three mile limit all shipwreck salvage required a State lease. State representatives were placed on each salvage vessel, monitoring activities and making sure that proper archeological procedures were followed. Outside the three mile limit was still a free-for-all, and although this was territorial waters, the Federal government had not yet become a factor in salvage operations. So in the summer of '66 the race was on by at least a dozen salvage groups to locate the *El Populo* and the *San Jose*.

The professional groups used small aircraft to circle the reefs, looking for the gray smudge on the bottom that would indicate a possible ballast pile. Dive boats crisscrossed the sand flats towing magnetometers that pinpoint shipwreck material lying as much as 15 feet below the sand. But the finding of the *Populo* was not by one of the professional salvage groups. The *Populo* was located by a group of four divers with little or no salvage experience. What they lacked in experience they more than made up for in dogged determination. This is their story.

September 1, 1966

Carl Fredericks had read the local accounts of the 1733 recoveries, and with some research background he knew the *Populo* had never been located. One of his co-workers at Air Lift International in Miami was an electronic superstar by the name of Lee Harding. Lee had worked up the circuit board for an underwater metal detector and was anxious to try it out on a wreck-site. Carl Ward was a Miami Beach policeman that had been diving galleon sites for about a year in the Florida

Keys. Bob McKay was an airline jockey for Eastern, with time on his hands between trips, and a desire to search for treasure on old Spanish galleons. It was a compatible group that found themselves searching the reefs through a glass window built into the hull of their 19' boat 1¹/₂ miles south of Pacific Reef light. Fredericks had a hunch the *Populo* might be nearby.

On a sun-filled day, water flat calm and crystal clear, a perfect day for bottom search, they all seemed to spot it at the same time! There were two large cannon lying on a sandy bottom in 32' of water near a large circular reef. As they circled the reef for a better look the shoreward side of the reef sloped gradually away to a sandy bottom. The seaward side had an abrupt face, and against it was a pile of ballast stone!

It was the first cannon wreck-site any of the group had ever seen—enough to get their adrenaline pumping as the excited divers checked over the pile. It was like mounting up and riding off in all directions. Each one found different things to shout about as they popped their heads above water, then back to the bottom. Taking bearings on several prominent landmarks, the group decided it was smart to leave the area before other salvage divers spotted them, until they could come back with equipment to start salvage work. All the way shoreward to Homestead Bayfront Park they talked over the possibilities that this could be the missing *Populo*. It was certainly the right area, and probably about the right size. It all depended upon what their salvage efforts turned up if indeed they had found the missing galleon. It had been a shot in the dark, a chance finding of what could possibly be an important wreck-site, as the group sized up their situation. In terms of equipment all they had was a 19' boat and suspect motor, a 3" suction dredge, and enough SCUBA tanks to keep them on the bottom about two hours each per day. They recognized that other salvage groups would be searching the area, and if they were spotted working the site the jig was up. It would be fair game for anyone to move in on them. Their opportunity to work this virgin wreck-site existed only as long as their ability to keep its location a secret.

It was a week later before they could return to the site, and it was unforgettable. First, it was extremely difficult to relocate. Five miles from land it is a problem locating and taking accurate bearings on anything. The best roadmap is the bottom of the ocean, but when underwater visibility is poor even that is of no help. After an hour of towing a diver behind the boat like a trolling piece of bait, they finally were able to spot the reef and the cannon. With air tanks on their backs they scouted the site from one end to the other before comparing notes. The ballast piles lay N to S against the face of the reef and was 70' long and 30' wide. The reef rose 10' above bottom, and on the north end lay deep gray silt and mud. On the south end, where the first two cannon were spotted, white sand stretched out into a bottom of eel grass. Another half moon reef lay several hundred yards away. They located three more cannon in the ballast pile, one of them much shorter than the others. The entire ballast pile lay in a patch of white sand a hundred feet in diameter. The reef that helped hide this wreck-site was no more than 150' long.

Before leaving that day they decided to raise the smaller cannon. It took a lot of struggling to get it into the boat, even though it was no more than $3\frac{1}{2}'$ long. The next day their excitement mounted even higher when they chipped away the coral encrustation and discovered their cannon was *bronze!* It had some distinctive markings that were later used to help identify their wreck-site as the *Populo.* Their reaction was spontaneous. Bronze cannon meant treasure ships. They were sure that there was treasure somewhere in the ballast pile.

In order to keep the site a secret no marker buoys were used. A lookout would always remain in the boat to warn of other boats coming close. Often entire days of operation would be shut down because a fishing boat had anchored a hundred yards away. Trips to the ballast pile were more often made during the week when fewer boats were working off the outer reefs. When aircraft would circle overhead the dredge was shut down, the hoses disconnected and thrown over the side. At first lobster fishermen became suspicious that these new divers could be raiding their traps. Every once in a while they would pass close aboard and look them over well. After the first few months their 19' boat became a part of the everyday local activity.

The fall of 1966 brought the group, and their families, closer together as they all shared the dream that their wreck held treasure somewhere amid the timbers and ballast. At first their efforts paid off in buckets full of cannon balls, grape shot, and lead musket balls. Enough to have them dub their pile the "Cannon Ball Wreck." Once in a while an unusual artifact was uncovered by the sand dredge. A seven inch silver plate with marks "N" and "O" on the bottom, many blue and white pieces of *Kang Hsi* porcelain, and a lot of pottery shards of olive jars . . . the utility containers of all the Spanish fleets. Initially their objective was to dredge test holes in a number of locations, and if treasure were found then expand the hole. But silver and gold eluded them. It was seven months before their first treasure coin was recovered, and then what a beauty! It was a full dated 1732 Pillar Dollar, not only extremely rare and valuable, but also positive proof that their vessel was the remains of a 1733 Plate Fleet galleon. With no other 1733 wrecks anywhere near this area they were now positive they had the *Populo*. The Pillar Dollar was the first round silver coin made by a screw press in the New World. One had recently brought $2500 at an auction in New Jersey. This recovery produced a new round of treasure fever, and moving a ton of ballast stone in a single day became suddenly a labor of love.

1967

The weather and Bob McKay's flying schedule kept the trips to the wreck-site limited as the weeks and months wore on. Lee Harding developed his new underwater detector and some "hot spots" were located that began to produce artifacts . . . as well as adding to the growing pile of cannon balls in Fredericks' back yard. But there were weeks on end when nothing was found, and just when patience and frustration began to show, the wreck would give up another Piece of Eight. They tried visualizing how the ship had struck the reef and sunk. Not being professionals, nor having worked a wreck-site before, they really had no idea whether the bow of the ship faced north or south. They knew that treasure was generally carried in the sterncastle, but was that at the end of the reef with the deep mud and silt, or to the south where the ballast stones disappeared into the sand and eel grass. This is where the first two cannon were found, but what part of the ship did they come from? Under the ballast they discovered two more large cannon making a total of six, plus the bronze mortar. Two small swivel guns were uncovered alongside the last two large cannon in the area where the hull section rested against the side of the reef. After some correspondence with Mendel Peterson of the Smithsonian Institute, a decision was made to try burrowing under the hull timbers to the keel. Gold and silver have a habit of working their way along the turn of the hull to the keel, but tunneling after it can become dangerous. The weakened timbers could give way and trap the diver with little hope of rescue before his air ran out. The risk seemed worth it so Fredericks and Ward started a tunnel that eventually turned into a trench as sand continued to cave in around them. Soon it was apparent that the weight of the ballast over the rotted timbers was too much. The stones had to be removed before they could go any deeper. It took about twelve hours of all hands moving rocks before they could continue with the trench. Soon about six feet of the keel lay exposed, but still no treasure. To dig further meant a lot more ballast would have to be removed and the '67 diving season was fast approaching the end. Some test holes were dug into the deep silt and mud at the north end. As soon as they started digging the visibility went to zero, so digging at that end went slowly. After a number of holes the only artifacts recovered were more cannon balls and grape shot. Test holes in the south end uncovered much more of the bottom timbers than they realized existed. It was when they began digging a trench along the hull lying against the reef that great artifacts were recovered. At first several wooden pulley blocks appeared, then a pair of bronze navigational dividers, a pair of scissors, several bronze bowls, an ivory tuning pin from a musical instrument, brass buckles, a granite milling stone, a vanilla bean jar, and three silver Pieces of Eight. It seemed like buckets full of pottery shards and pieces of blue and white Chinese *Kang Hsi* porcelain had been collected over the past year of salvage. Carl Ward began putting some of the pieces together, first with a pottery bowl about 4" in diameter, then with a porcelain cup. Hopes of finding an intact porcelain cup after a hurricane sank this ship seemed impossible, so the task was to piece one together. After about 20 carefully selected pieces that fit together, the porcelain cup lacked only a small triangular piece to make it complete. Carl kept his eye out for the missing piece. With these latest finds the treasure fever was with them again. It was decided to move more ballast from the hull and continue the trench along the keel. Several weeks later, with much more of the keel exposed, they still found nothing.

Hurricane "Beulah" churned in from the Lesser Antilles and cut diving short as bad weather prevailed over the Keys. The year wound down with only an occasional trip to the site in spite of high waves and poor visibility. But it had been a rewarding year.

1968

Their last year on the site found the group on alternate days working first one end of the wreck-site, then the other. They had no sure way of knowing which end was the stern where the treasure had been stored, and so far they certainly had not found it. In spite of their precaution in not buoying the site, several boats full of divers had located them while they were working the bottom. It would be only a matter of time before the salvage community would know about the location of the *Populo*. There now seemed an urgency to complete the salvage before this happened. Much of the site still remained unexplored because of the deep sand and their limited equipment. Lee Harding had put together a hookah, or breathing compressor, so the SCUBA tanks quickly became past history. Time on the bottom was now limited by daylight or the weather. A marker was placed near the reef, in line with a distant spar buoy, saving them time in searching for the reef on each trip. As a result they began to dig a number of test holes, not expanding any unless something of value was recovered. Several more wooden blocks were recovered in the sand at the south end, as well as a large part of a pottery communion bowl 6¹/₂" in diameter with exquisite design in relief on the inside. Carl Ward one day came to the surface shouting as if he had been attacked by a shark. When the excitement died down, it turned out that he had located the last small triangular piece of the porcelain cup.

The end of the treasure quest came during the month of September. Other salvagers had now located the wreck-site, and one day as they were passing through Black Caesar's Creek they noticed a cabin cruiser towing a large object slung under several 55 gallon drums. The object turned out to be one of their cannon. When they reached the site they were astounded at finding all their cannon missing, and large areas of the hull exposed where others had been digging. As they sat in their boat over the *Populo* it was truly a moment of sadness. They had the wreck-site to themselves for nearly two years, and had recovered some remarkable artifacts. Never the treasure they had imagine, because the piles of silver and gold were never there to begin with. The *Populo* carried no registered treasure. But what the *Populo* did do was provide each with an experience they would never forget. The companionship that had survived months of frustration and hardship, and the memories of a successful hunt. Although not the pot of gold at the end of the rainbow, it was treasure nonetheless.

*Carl Ward with
3¹/₂' Populo
bronze cannon*

*Photo Credit -
Ernie Richards*

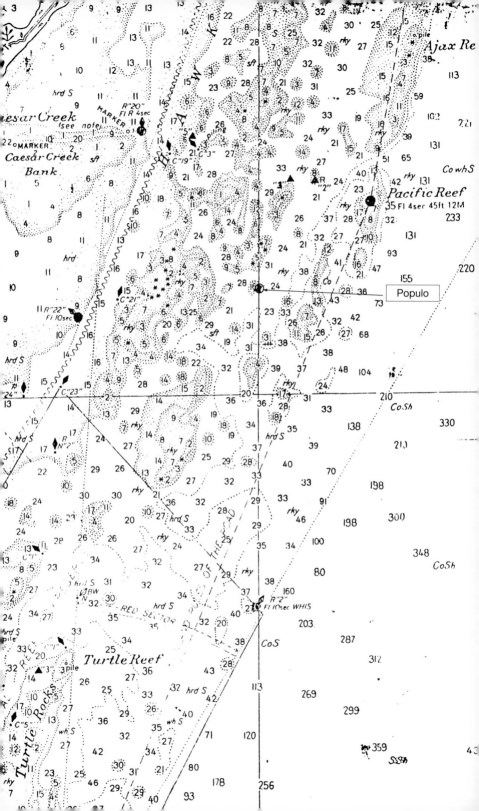

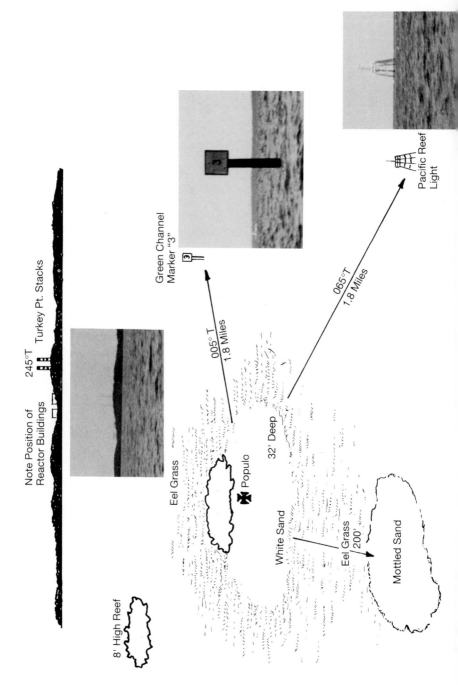

Note Position of
Reactor Buildings

Turkey Pt. Stacks

245°T

Green Channel
Marker "3"

Pacific Reef
Light

005° T
1.8 Miles

065°T
1.8 Miles

32' Deep

Eel Grass

Populo

White Sand

Eel Grass
200'

Mottled Sand

8' High Reef

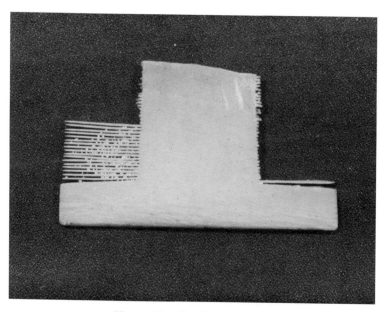

"Ivory Lice Comb" — Populo
Photo Credit: E. Richards

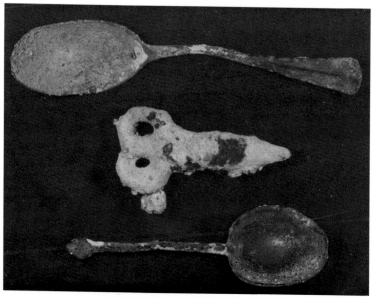

"Spoons and a Pair of Scissors" — Populo
Photo Credit: E. Richards

Clay Communion Bowl for Shipboard Services.
Photo Credit: E. Richards

Divers that located and savlaged the Populo. L to R Carl Freder-icks, Bob McKay, Lee Harding, Carl Ward. Photo Credit: Fredericks

Bottle and Lead Box — Populo
Photo Credit: E. Richards

Porcelain Kang Hsi Cups — Populo
Photo Credit: E. Richards

Fragments of a large Kang Hsi Porcelain Bowl
Photo Credit: E. Richards

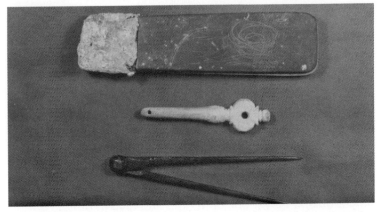

Honing Stone, ivory tuning pin from a musical instrument, and brass navigational dividers. Photo Credit: E. Richards

"Pillar Dollar similar to one recovered from the Populo."
Photo Credit: E. Richards

Chapter II
HMS Winchester 1695

Loran: 43191.9, 62216.7
Latitude: 24° 51' 10"
Longitude: 80° 44' 00"

It was a time of confused warfare in the New World. With the establishment of her colonies along the North American coastline, *Britannia* had become the undisputed leader in maritime commerce. The war of the Grand Alliance pitted England against France, and for the first time found her allied with Spain. But at the same time King William's War broke out with the French trying to take New York, and England attacking Quebec City. It meant all the active fighting naval squadrons that England could muster for sea duty were dispatched to the New World to maintain the umbilical cord of ships that tied the English empire together. *HMS Winchester* and *HMS Dunkirk*, along with a *refuerzo* formed a squadron stationed in Port Royal, Jamaica. Their sole purpose was to harass the French and take as many prizes as they could.

But it was a time in English naval history when long terms of sea duty saw living conditions aboard their warships deteriorating. A time when scurvy and dysentery were more deadly than a French broadside. In one instance an admiral of a squadron and all but one of his captains died of disease during a cruise. And it was so with *Winchester*. Her cruise was completed, and she was scheduled to return home in company with *Dunkirk* and a French brigantine that had been captured. Her captain, as well as some of her crew, had become sick and were transferred ashore in Jamaica. Captain John Soule was put in command and the three ships left Port Royal. Within ten days the squadron rounded the southern coast of Cuba and began to ride the Gulf Stream as it curved the scimitar of the Florida Keys. But scurvy had become rampant on board *Winchester*. The original crew of over 300 men were caught up in the disease that swept over the ship. It struck without warning. Bleeding gums, livid skin patches, and generalized exhaustion, all due to a lack of vitamin C. Crewmen were dying by the hour, and as the ships sailed within hailing distance of each other, the officers and crew aboard *Dunkirk* watched in dismay as the ritual of dropping bodies sewn in canvas over the side in burial at sea continued day and night. It reached a point when exhaustion of the remaining crew would not allow them to put the bodies in bags, but let them slide over the side with little more than a final salute. *Dunkirk* was certain that a plague was running rampant on her sister ship.

On September 23, 1695 by nightfall the ships had sighted Cape Florida north by $^{1}/_{2}$ east (Cape Florida in that day meant any part of the lower east coast of Florida. Early English charts gave that name to a promontory known today as Upper Sound Point, off Key Largo) a distance of three leagues. The squadron tacked to the SE to take advantage of the wind from the ENE. On board *Winchester* the decimated crew had only eight able-bodied seamen on deck besides the Master Andrew Mallard and the 1st Lieutenant John Hisket. "The rest being sick to ye number of 50 men and boys or thereabout." Even Captain Soule had come down with scurvy. By 8 P.M. the wind had veered to the southeast and the ships close-hauled to the NE. With the reefs so close at hand the lead line was thrown every hour, and at 11 P.M. no bottom was found at 75 fathoms. Their course was now parallel to the jagged reefs that marked the edge of the Gulf Stream, and unknowingly less than a mile of open water now separated them.

At midnight the wind again veered to the east and the Commodore, Captain Butler, on the *Dunkirk* gave the signal to begin tacking back towards the center of the Bahama Channel and deeper water. *Winchester,* with only a few men to man the sails, ran about three-quarters of a mile before she had worn four points. Suddenly the ship "struck a ledge of rocks which lye about four leagues to ye north of ye Cape, and about ye like distance from ye shore." Within a half hour's time the ship had bilged her bottom and Mallard realized the ship was lost. A yawl was put over the side and they found the counter current to the southwest was so strong around their ship that with four men rowing they could hardly make way. With a sounding lead they found seven feet of depth over the reef they had struck, and sixteen feet to the stern.

In the morning the *Dunkirk*, standing offshore, ordered the prize brigantine "Under pain of death" to go alongside *Winchester* and save as many souls as they could. *Dunkirk* was afraid that what had plagued the crew might also affect them. The brigantine transferred those that were still alive from the *Winchester*. Captain Soule, however, was gravely injured in the transfer. He later died as what was left of the squadron made their way northward. He was buried on the beach in Virginia.

For 245 years the pile of cannon and ballast stone lay undisturbed some 25 miles south of present day Miami. Then, two black fishermen, Sam Lynch and Jacob Munroe of Miami, spotted the cannon lying on the outer reef near Key Largo. One day while fishing near Elliot Key they ran out of gas for their outboard motor and poled ashore near where Charlie Brookfield lived at Ledbury Lodge. Charlie was a well-known local historian, and on this day he had gas for their engine, ice for their fish, and a hot meal. The next day they both came to Charlie with a great show of secrecy, and said they had seen a large number of cannon at a certain spot on the reefs. They knew Charlie had an interest in old wrecks, and if they might be compensated they would show him the place.

Stories of sunken treasure had always intrigued Brookfield. A neighbor of his, John Sanders, while building his home on Elliot Key in 1898 had found a cache of buried treasure. The *Hubbard* had wrecked at the entrance to the channel leading to Black Caesar's Creek in the early 1700's, and the *Ledbury* had been stranded by a hurricane and burned in 1769 near where his lodge had been built. Each had stories yarned ashore about buried loot that made the fires of treasure fever burn brightly. Charlie's hope had always been to locate a treasure-laden Spanish galleon, and piles of cannon spelled that possibility. He went after it. The two black fishermen were able to relocate the cannon at the edge of a finger reef not more than a mile south of Carysfort Lighthouse. It was hoped that the cannon would be bronze, an excellent possibility then that the wreck was a Spanish treasure galleon. But, upon closer inspection, the cannon that lay like matchsticks near the base of the reef were made of iron. Still, it was possible that a ship with this many cannon could yield historical artifacts, and information leading to its identification.

Brookfield mounted a salvage expedition that included raising some of the cannon for preservation. An ocean-going barge, the *Charles W. Baird*, aground on White Bank not far away, was used as shelter during the diving operation. The year was 1938 and although hard hat diving was the only means of salvage, it did provide some results. The reef had cemented many of the artifacts to the coral and covered them with a natural growth. Without metal detectors they were never recovered. But cannon balls, musket balls, anchors, and some small arms were pried from the bottom. In sand holes they retrieved several silver and copper coins, parts of a gold watch, and a silver porringer (two handled soup bowl). Amazingly, in a conglomerate protected by coral growth, a small part of a page from a prayer book was found—the "litany of Loreto," written in Latin!

Identification of the wreck-site as the remains of the *Winchester* was accomplished by several artifacts. The cannon, when cleaned, were discovered to have a Tudor Rose crown cast in relief on the first re-inforce. The letters T.W. and H. appeared on the end of the trunnions. Finally, a copper coin was recovered, and when cleaned revealed the seated figure of Britannia—and the date 1694. Counting the number of cannon on the site gave the salvagers some idea of the size of their wreck, as well as the strong possibility that it was English. With this information, a letter was written to the British Admiralty asking if one of their ships had sunk near the Florida Keys some time after 1694, and carrying at least 48 cannon. Within a few weeks they had their answer. Their site was *HMS Winchester*, a fourth rate ship carrying 60 cannon, lost at the head of the *Martires* in September 1695. The founders mark T.W. were probably those of Thomas Westerne who operated a gun foundry at Ashburnham in Sussex from 1669-88. It was worth the salvage effort. They had their answer, and some great artifacts to preserve and commemorate this once proud ship. After the publicity and the salvage operations ceased, the cannon seemed to mount up and ride off in all directions. Several are still located on Lignum Vitae Key, just below Tavernier Key. During the war Art McKee raised many of them, and they were melted down for scrap iron. At least one of the cannon was shipped to England, where it was melted down and combined with other iron and steel being used to build the new English warship *HMS Winchester*.

In the 1960's charter boat captain Bobby Klein dived the site, and, chipping through the coral bottom, he was able to recover some great artifacts. These were featured in the December, 1977, issue of *National Geographic* and included a number of brass navigational dividers, silver plates, buckles, tableware, and an ivory sundial. In 1985 Bobby re-visited the site and was surprised to find a small mound of over 300 cannon balls and some ship's fittings up behind the reef where no artifacts should have been scattered. Then, after some diligent research, he learned that one night Art McKee had gotten upset with some of the other divers (or possibly Charlie Brookfield) and had dumped everything they had recently found over the side of the *Charles W. Baird!*

Today the wreck-site lies within the boundary of John Pennecamp Park and is protected from further salvage. But there is little left to be seen anyway, for the cannon have long since vanished, and the ballast pile has become part of the third finger reef south of Carysfort in 16 feet of water. Only the history remains of this once proud English ship-of-the-line.

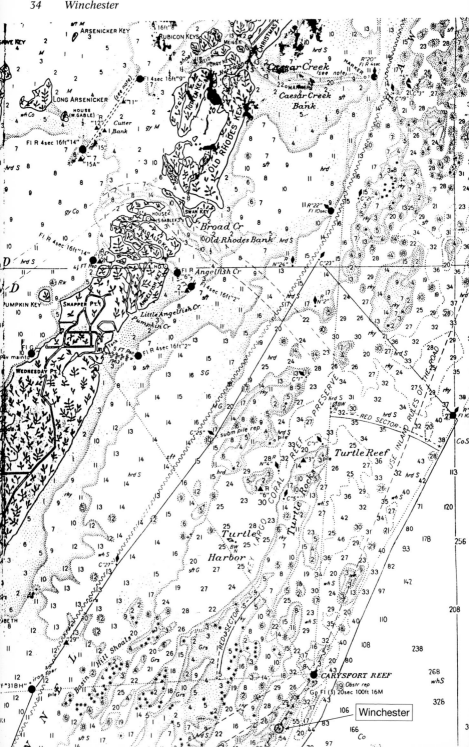

Winchester

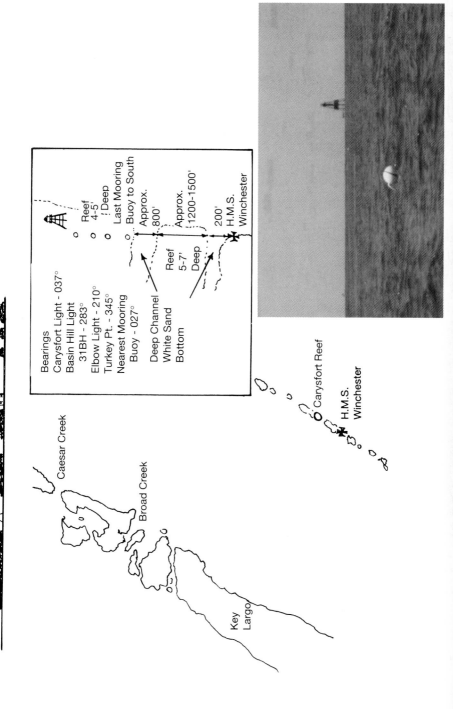

Bearings
Carysfort Light - 037°
Basin Hill Light
  31BH - 283°
Elbow Light - 210°
Turkey Pt. - 345°
Nearest Mooring
  Buoy - 027°

Deep Channel
White Sand
Bottom

Reef
4-5'
Deep

Last Mooring
Buoy to South

Approx.
800'

Approx.
1200-1500'

Reef
5-7'
Deep

200'
H.M.S.
Winchester

Caesar Creek

Broad Creek

Key Largo

Carysfort Reef

H.M.S.
Winchester

Top Row — Brass Pull and 4 Brass Buttons. Center — Money Bag Seal and Split Musket Shot. Bottom — Knife Band, Musket Flint Magnifying Glass Rim. Photo Credit: E. Richards

Ivory Sundial — Winchester. Ref: National Geographic Dec. 1977.
Photo Credit: E. Richards

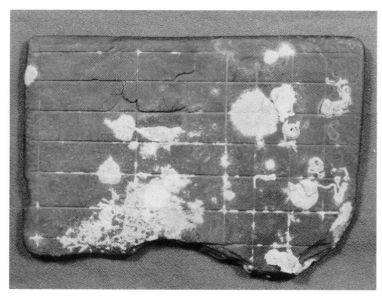

Slate for Logging Speed Wind and Depth — Winchester
Photo Credit: E. Richards

Two Barrel Spigots and the top and bottom of a powder flask — Winchester. *Photo Credit: E. Richards*

Silver Plate and spoon — Winchester. *Photo Credit: E. Richards*

Clay pipe — Winchester 1695. *Photo Credit: E. Richards*

Two silver plates — Winchester. *Photo Credit: E. Richards*

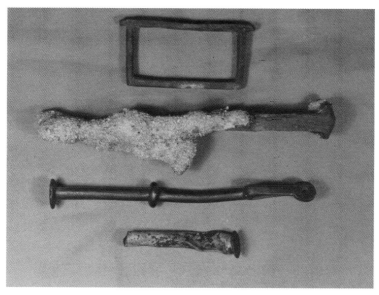

Belt buckle spike, pie crust cutter, brass seal (TM). Photo Credit: E. Richards

"Captain Bob Klein" — Winchester Salvor. Photo Credit: Bob Weller

The author and his wife, with an encrusted flintlock pistol he recovered from the Spanish Plate Fleet.

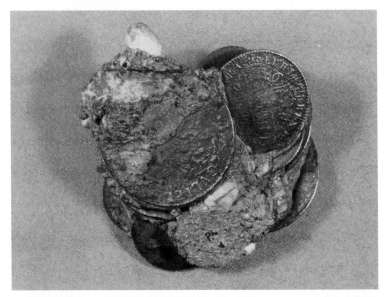

A conglomerate of encrusted coins - English, the latest date 1694.

Photo Credit: E. Richards

Chapter III
San Jose 1728-1733

"Parker"

Alias: San José de las Animas
Loran: 14108.4, 43268.8
Latitude: 24° 55' 41'''
Longitude: 80° 28' 51"

The launch moved easily around the lee of the island catching a brisk easterly wind, and as the ocean swells sent spray over the gunnels the occupants huddled closer to the center console. The camera cases marked "CBS" were quickly covered with canvas and captain Gene Geh remarked "We've got four miles to go, so everyone get comfortable." Behind the launch, at the end of a 50' towing hawser, rode a 19' fiberglass boat loaded with a strange cargo of sloshing water-filled containers. It was an unusual entourage that would mark the end to one of the darkest hours in Florida salvage history.

Soon the red buoy that marked the grave of the *San Jose* bobbed over the top of a wave, and Geh throttled back, letting the launch settle into the wind. The small boat being towed was pulled alongside and bearded treasure salvor Tom Gurr stepped on board. As CBS cameramen focused on the scene Tom announced, "In protest of the deplorable political situation that currently exists within the Florida Department of Archives, History and Records Management Division, I hereby return to the sea from whence it came, artifacts and treasure recovered from the *San Jose!*" With that he reached into the plastic container he held and began to throw identifiable treasures into the sea. With the cameras rolling he held aloft encrusted flintlock pistols, swords, pewter platters, and threw them overboard. As he worked from one side of the boat to the other suddenly the small boat broached between two waves and began taking water over the side and stern. With the television cameras filming away the unexpected happened . . . the boat sank out from under Gurr! As he swam over to

the launch, the rough seas finished the job of returning treasure back to the *San Jose.*

The *San Jose* was built in the New England colonies during
the 1727-28 period. The American oak timbers made a stout
hull, and trees that grew straight and tall in the Carolinas were
sought after by all builders of ships to serve as masts. English-
made blocks and dead-eyes, as well as other rigging, made the
Jose a choice addition to the young colonies merchant marine.
It was named *Saint Joseph* and was originally destined for the
trade between England and the colonies. By 1730 the Spanish
were in search of merchant vessels to carry the plate fleet treasure from the New World back to Spain. The newly constructed *Saint Joseph* suited their needs as a heavily armed galleon
to carry treasure and also protect the smaller *naos* on the long
journey back. They purchased the vessel, renaming her the *Sn
Joseph Y Las Animas . . . San Jose* for short. Even the English
silver dinner service was included in the purchase. Within
months the *San Jose* was in Spain being outfitted as one of the
four larger galleons that would accompany the Nueva Espana
fleet to Vera Cruz. The fleet of 21 ships set sail in August,
1732, reaching the leeward islands within 50 days . . . weather
permitting. From there it was clear sailing across the relatively
calm Caribbean to Vera Cruz on the Mexican coast.

Until the Spanish Plate Fleets arrived, the little town of
Vera Cruz lay in a state of hibernation. Little if anything went
on, and few inhabitants remained there because of the fever
attributed to the surrounding marshlands. The village of Jala-
pa, 50 miles inland, provided much of the labor in loading the
treasure aboard the galleons upon arrival. Once the fleet was
anchored in the protected harbor the celebration began, and
Vera Cruz was transformed into a bustling beehive of activity.
Merchants from the surrounding towns and villages made
their way to the auction to bid on the European goods being
off-loaded from these high-masted freight trains of the sea. At
the same time silver mined in the New Biscay province of
Central Mexico, Zacatecas mines of San Martin and Tenescal-
tetec were shipped by mule train down the winding paths that

lead from the mountainous terrain to the flat lands along the coast. The coinage from the Mexico mints, including the first "Pillar Dollars" (screw press coins dated 1732) ever struck in the New World were placed in wooden, lead-lined chests, approximately three feet long, two feet wide, one foot deep. Each chest contained about 3,000 Pieces of Eight. These were also loaded on the backs of pack mules for the long journey from the mints to the seacoast. From Acapulco came porcelain *Kang Hsi* cups, bowls, and "ginger jars," carried by the Manila Galleon fleet across the Pacific from the trade fair held in the Philippines. The streets of Vera Cruz soon filled with peddlers and prostitutes as the feria or fair began. It would last for weeks, depending upon how long it took to send the word to the Spanish outposts that the fleet had arrived, and for the treasure to find its way to the coast. In the meantime the sailors had an opportunity to stretch their sea-legs, and do a little trading of their own. For many reasons the 1732 fair stretched into the spring of 1733 before the fleet was able to raise anchor and begin the perilous voyage along the coast of Mexico towards the port of Havana.

When the *Jose* arrived in Havana its cargo holds held a representative sample of the wealth of the New World. Once there, although seemingly loaded to the gunwhales, more tobacco and exotic woods were added to the cargo holds. Even the open decks were crowded with chickens and livestock to provide fresh meat for the long journey back to Spain. More passengers were taken on board, and the heavily ladened ship slowly took its place in line as the fleet moved out of Havana harbor at sunrise on July 13, 1733. The dull booming of cannon on the parapets above the harbor seemed to be a suitable send-off for the fleet long-delayed past a safe window of time from hurricanes. And a *huracán* was already less than 400 miles to the east and bearing down on the unsuspecting ships.

Captain D. Cristobal Fernandez Franco was assigned a position near the center of the fleet so that *Jose's* cannon would help persuade Privateers along the Bahama Banks to think twice before attempting a raid on the smaller and slower *naos* that stretched out for several miles as the ships made their way into the north flowing channel. The fleet tacked westward toward the *Cabeza de Los Martires,* and were nearing the low slung mangroves when the hurricane struck. The ships scattered before the winds but within sight of the *Jose* was the *Capitana, Herrera, Murgia, El Terri, Tres Puentes, San Pedro* and the *El Infante. Infante* had struck the outer edge of the reefs to the north on Little Conch Reef and 20 foot waves were already battering her to pieces when the *San Jose* swept between Little Conch Reef and Davis Reef to the south. Even though she missed the dragons teeth she came down hard on her stern in the sand flats that stretched towards Hawks Channel. Her stern section shattered, then separated from the main hull. Within 200 yards the hull settled to the bottom in 31 feet of water, her bow to seaward and the gaping remainder of her sterncastle facing shoreward.

After the hurricane passed to the west, survivors were found floating in the area, clinging to boxes, spars, or anything that would remain above water. Many of the survivors were picked up by the *El Africa* and reached Havana only days after leaving. A proud ship the *San Jose,* lost on the Florida *Martires.*

Tom Gurr was a successful engineer with the Florida Flood Control District in Miami. As the salvage of the 1733 Spanish Plate Fleet by modern day salvors got into full swing in the early 60's the local newspapers were running daily accounts of the salvage of each site as it was located. Photos of cannon, flintlock pistols, arquebuses, swords, and a few coins was enough to stir the restlessness in anyone that ever dreamed of sunken treasures. Gurr was one of those that felt he had to give it a go. He resigned his job, and along with several associates, went searching for a suitable salvage boat. They found the *Parker,* tied to a dock on the Miami River. At 90' in length, it had a great 30' beam for deck-mounting equipment, and an 8' draft as a stable platform in moderate seas. The boat had been built for pilot duty in New York harbor in the

1890's, and retired after WWII. Some time in the 40's it was taken out of retirement, re-engined with diesel power, and put back into service as a lugger on the Chesapeake. Once again in retirement in the middle 60's as a houseboat it ran aground off Key Largo and Olin Frick became its owner as salvager. Gurr bought the *Parker* and his crew went to work repairing the dry rot that seemed to have taken up residence in the hull planking. They deck mounted a large air compressor, and built a diving platform along her port side. With all the equipment needed to go a-salvaging on board, the boat was ready by the summer of 1967 . . . and so were the divers.

Their shake-down cruise was the "Pillar Dollar" wreck-site off upper Key Largo. Art Sapp and Bobby Savage had located the site earlier and had recovered a number of 1760 Pillar Dollars. After several weeks on the site, and with nothing of value recovered, the *Parker* was headed south to the Coffin Patch wreck-site of the *Sn Ygnacio*, and some of Tom's associates headed back to regular paying jobs. The *Ygnacio* was scattered shoreward over several miles from where the ballast pile and cannon lay, and although a great many magnificent artifacts had been recoverd along its path, it proved to be slim pickings for Gurr. He heard of a virgin wreck-site near Hen & Chickens light, about ¹/₂ - 1 mile seaward in line with Alligator Light, and in time located it where Hawks Channel sand and eel grass deepens to 22 feet of water. This wreck had cannon scattered over a large ballast pile, and although not a great deal of interesting artifacts were recovered they did located a 2¹/₂ foot bronze blunderbuss rail gun. The site was then nicknamed the *"Blunderbuss Wreck."* Gurr raised 28 iron cannon to the deck of the *Parker* and headed for dockage behind Key Colony Beach in Marathon. This was heady stuff, the encrusted cannon and artifacts they had recovered were real signs of treasure, but the *Blunderbuss Wreck* had probably sunk in the 1740's and Tom wanted part of the 1733 silver plate fleet.

The summer salvage season of 1968 was just getting underway, so with the deck load of cannon safely stowed away in an underwater depository, Gurr shifted his attention to the

1733 wreck-site of the *El Infante*. This site had been giving up treasure since Watkins and the crew of the *Buccaneer* worked it in 1957. It was an easy wreck to locate, on the front slope of Little Conch Reef, and soon the *Parker* was on a four point anchorage over the ballast pile. As salvage operations began the thought still nagged at Gurr that most of the treasure had already been recovered from this site. First by the Spanish, and later by modern day salvors Watkins, Klein, Hamilton, Weller, and Meylach. His salvage vessel and equipment were expensive, and his financial reserves were running low. He had financial backers available, but without treasure to whet the appetite, even they would soon be history. He needed a virgin treasure wreck of the 1733 fleet. From the British Museum of History he had gotten a copy of the chart locating the various 1733 plate fleet wreck-sites along the reefs of Florida. But the charts were vague and inaccurate. It was one that had been available to the previous salvors for several years, and although interpretation had helped them locate many of the sites, one of the major galleons, the *San Jose* . . . like the golden condor, had eluded everyones' efforts. It didn't seem to be where the charts said it was, there near the edge of Hawks Channel. In that area flat sand seemed to stretch forever, and ballast mounds leave lumps in the sand even when the sand is deep. With a great deal of cross-referencing to land-marks, Tom laid out a grid of approximately $1/2$ mile and felt confident the *Jose* had to lie somewhere within that area. Next he contacted treasure salvor Mel Fisher and offered a piece of the action if he could borrow one of his "Fay Feild" magnetometers. Mel was always a lucky gambler, and he was "in."

With the *Parker* firmly anchored over the *Infante* a mile from the grid, the *"Revenooer,"* appropriately a former admiral's gig, was used to tow the magnetometer. The search was on. In the gig as it crisscrossed the area were Tom, Jim King, George Hanses, Dick Williams, and Rudy Paladino. It was July 15, 1968 —235 years from the day the *San Jose* sank, that the proton magnetometer sang out with a big anomaly indicating a mass of metal on the bottom. The divers piled over the side expecting to see a ballast pile, cannons, anchors, but there was nothing except an expanse of eel grass and white sand. The water was a gin clear 31 feet in depth, and as the divers searched in all directions nothing was visible above the bottom. Back on the *Revenooer* they crossed the area and began dropping buoys. The anomaly seemed to be the strongest at the edge of a patch of eel grass, so Rudy Paladino swam to the bottom with the shaft of a spear gun and began probing into the sand. About three feet deep he heard that distinct click when metal strikes ballast stone. Pay dirt! It was an exciting afternoon as thoughts of salvaging the *Infante* suddenly evaporated. The crew raised all four *Parker* anchors and headed for the bobbing buoys that marked the hot spot. Once again the anchors were set like a spider web, and the air compressor fired up. With 6 inch diameter air-lifts probing through the sand the ballast stones were soon uncovered. Across the pile there seemed to be cannon everywhere. Tom was certain it was the *San Jose*. He had known Mendel Peterson of the Smithsonian Institute for years, and as soon as Tom was certain he had the *Jose* he called Mendel with the exciting news. Mendel expressed a desire to work with Tom as the wreck was uncovered, doing serious archeological studies. Tom agreed to stop all work if Mendel could come to Florida within a week. Peterson made it, along with a group of archeologists including artist Peter Copeland, and George Fisher from the National Park Services. For the next several weeks the group sketched the site, measured timbers and took underwater bearings. Many of the artifacts were sketched *in situ*, others on board the *Parker* after they had been cleaned and cataloged. While this was in progress the magnetometer picked up another large anomaly 200 yards to the SE. As the air-lifts moved sand away five more cannon and the large 21 foot rudder of the *San Jose* appeared. After that it seemed each day brought new surprises. George Hosford was working seaward of the ballast when he uncovered a complete stack of silver plates, and an equal number of forks and spoons. On the back of each plate was clearly labeled the maker's mark "Buckby and Hamilton, London England 1722." Ray Manieri came out from under the hull timbers, his fingers covered in gold rings, some with large emeralds that had been designed to fill a senorita's heart with fire. A complete barber's kit was recovered near the edge of the ballast, complete with several bone-handled razors, scissors, and a lice comb. Lloyd Gurr, Tom's son, was always fanning away in the most difficult places that the other divers could not squeeze into and he found gold, enough to be dubbed "Goldnose." Soon the deck of the *Parker* was covered with artifacts. Several flintlock pistols, an array of dress swords and boarding cutlasses, *Kang Hsi* porcelain cups and bowls, many gold rings, a single gold coin, buckles, buttons, a number of glazed pottery figurines, and finally a unique glass figurine of a cat emerged from the ballast pile intact. The artifact that created the most conversation was the skull. It was recovered under some of the ship's timbers, near a spiked cannon that had been carried as ballast. The skull was aptly named "Jose." Because of its state of preservation it was suggested that this was the body of an important person being transported back to Spain. Divers helping to bring up all the loot included John Nowland, Jack Cosgrove, Tom Gardner, Pete Roe, Carl Raffa, Jim Bell, Scotty Campbell, Ray Manieri, Henry Taylor, Chuck Mitchell, Larry Antus, Kip Porter, Bernie Smith, and the author Bob Weller.

The coordination between the archeologists and the salvors was both cordial and a lot of fun, and it lasted three months. Then it was time for the Smithsonian people to head back north. The salvage work continued in full swing, but dark clouds were on the Tallahassee horizon. In dealing with the Smithsonian Institute, the National Park Service, Federal offices because the ship lay outside three mile territorial waters, Tom had bypassed the State of Florida officials. Now with all the publicity, there was a tempest in a teapot brewing. The State claimed the *San Jose* was within their territorial waters which they indicated extended three miles beyond the outer reefs. They sent their archeologist Carl Clausen to investigate. When Clausen approached the *Parker* anchored over the site he was refused permission to board. Gurr stated he was in international waters and held a salvage masters license to operate in those waters. When Clausen insisted on boarding, shots were fired over his head. That ended the day's confrontation and set the tenor of the State-Salvor relationship to follow. The following day a Coast Guard cutter appeared alongside the *Parker,* and with guns drawn and ready they boarded. It had been reported that the *Parker* was being used as a drop station for Cuban weapons. When none were found, apologies were made, and the cutter left. A week later Gurr had to go ashore for supplies, and as he stepped off the small launch he was promptly arrested by the Monroe County Sheriff's department. It was October 1968 . . . and it was all downhill after that. Tom Gurr contended that his civil rights were being violated. The State claimed the *San Jose* was within their territorial waters. In January 1969 Federal Judge William Mehrtens ordered Tom to turn over all artifacts in his possession to the State of Florida until it could be determined exactly where the *San Jose* was located. This ended Gurr's salvage operation, and to add to the frustration the *Parker* sank alongside its dock in Marathon.

Without a boat, crew, or financial backing, Tom busied himself with a marine business. During the summer of '69 Kip Wagner approached him with the possibility of filming a commercial movie on the *Jose.* Tom agreed, and during the summer the salvage vessel *Grifon* dusted the wreck off from stem to stern with its blowers. Notable salvagers Harry Cannon, Lou Ullian, Dan Thompson and Bob Marx completed the movie by the end of the summer, recovering a few artifacts in the process, and the *Jose* again was covered by drifting sand.

For the next several years Gurr worked at other things but the *San Jose* was never out of his thoughts. The fact that the sterncastle had landed solidly 200 yards to the seaward of the main ballast pile, dumping its rudder and five cannon, made him wonder if there wasn't treasure dumped at the same time. His crew had never made a serious salvage effort in this area and the more he thought about it the more it bugged him.

When a financial group with limited capital approached him in the spring of 1972 he jumped at the opportunity. "Undersea Mining" was formed and a salvage boat named *Capitana* was quickly outfitted with blowers to work the deep sand. By mid-year they were operational and back on the site, this time in a four point anchorage over the rudder area. As six to eight feet of sand and eel grass billowed away a hard packed sand bottom appeared. On this bottom lay rigging, dead-eyes, cargo hooks, and a hemp rope that wove its way around the bottom and through some of the rigging. The rope disintegrated at the touch, but one day while Tom was uncovering a section he noticed it turned downward and disappeared into the hard bottom! This hard packed sand could hardly be chipped with a knife, yet there had to be something underneath. In the past it had been assumed that this was the final hard bottom. Tom had the Capitana moved over the spot, and for the next hour the blower directed the prop thrust of water at the bottom of the hole. When the divers finally went down to check out the bottom of the hard pan they found the crust, almost 18 inches thick, had been broken through - and at the bottom of the new hole lay the glitter of gold! A gold bell, gold rings, jewelry, stacks of silver plates, religious medallions, gold brooches, treasures they had never expected to see. These were possibly the personal effects of the wealthy passengers on board and ship's officers. As the hole was expanded in the days that followed a great many new artifacts were uncovered including an intact *Kang Hsi* porcelain ginger jar, and a larger number of screw press type "Pillar Dollars" dated 1732. It seemed the artifacts were everywhere under the layer of hardpan, and the hardpan stretched the 200 yards NW to the ballast pile and at least that distance seaward where Hosford had recovered the silver plates. Just when the salvage of the treasure looked too good to be true, the financial budget depleted. Gurr decided to approach the State of Florida, Department of Records and Management, in an attempt to get his share in the division of the 1968 recoveries. With 75% share of the treasure it would be much easier to arrange further financing, or sell some of the treasure so he could keep his crew working. The State of Florida had other ideas. Much of the treasure Tom had recovered in '68 had already been cleaned and put on display at several locations. The State had seemingly already absorbed the entire treasure into their inventory. After three months of seriously trying to negotiate with Senator Robert Williams who represented the Department of Archives, all negotiations broke down. Williams refused to answer phone calls or meet with Gurr and they reached an impasse. On that note the '73 diving season faded away, and a frustrated Tom Gurr called his friend Jed Duval, a CBS official in Washington, and announced his intention to throw back into the ocean what treasures he had left from the *San Jose*. A film crew was dispatched and recorded the end of a dream, a dream of hope, fulfillment, and frustration. But the dream lives on, and somewhere on the site of the *San Jose* lies treasure still to be recovered.

Recoveries by the Spanish in 1733
231,397 pesos, 2 *reales* in silver and effects. The owners of the *San Jose* were charged for the salvage by the divers at a rate of 3 pesos, 8 centavos per 100 *pesos*. Leather bags of conchineal, indigo, cow hides, brown sugar, boxes of candy and chocolate were ruined by immersion and not salvaged.

Recoveries by the **Parker** - 1968

242 silver coins	4 silver buttons
1 copper coin	1 gold one escudo coin
1 bronze-gold ring with stones	4 high carat gold rings
3 bronze gold friendship rings	5 high carat gold ring fragments
13 bronze gold rings	2 brass weights and staff scale
	1 glass figurine of a cat

Bayonet and swords - San Jose

27 miniature clay figurines . . . tonalaware
2 ivory tuning keys
5 broken clay pipe bowls
6 broken clay pipe stems
4 intact pottery bowls
1 intact pottery cup
1 clay container
1 broken talisman
1 broken ivory fan
22 buckles
1 brass hinge
12 keys
2 pewter buttons
1 shoe snap
2 brass handle knives
1 ivory letter opener broken
3 candelabra broken
1 brass door knob
2 pewter ink wells
2 padlocks with keys
1 pocket knife
1 silver snuff box, shell design

San Jose—*Miniature clay figurines*

1 barbers kit, complete with razors, combs in leather pouch
1 pewter container
2 brass pulleys
1 bag of silver fragments
2 leather shoe soles
1 bayonet
2 sword handles + section
of sword blade
1 sounding lead
2 brass trigger guards
1 bronze medallion
1 sword intact
1 large intact olive jar
2 grinding wheels, stone
1 lead pump dated 1728
with bronze check value

Large intact olive jar

Parker Recoveries on **San Jose** - 1969
81 silver coins
1 pillar dollar 1732
2 clay figurines
33 silver plates
2 sections of rosary, 11 beads
in each section
1 silver shaker
1 intact olive jar
1 silver medallion
1 silver ring
9 silver objects
1 roll of lead sheathing
1 clump of cannon balls
2 lead scupper pipes
1 exploding hollow cannon ball
3 lead water line numerals
3 pieces of lead numbers
5 gold rings and a gold fragment
1 encrusted ring
1 grinding *metate*
15 olive jar shards
1 silver fork
1 gold seal (TA)
4 bronze gold rings
2 silver rings
1 silver buckle
1 bundle of leather
2 buttons, pewter
1 piece of mother of pearl
4 bone handled knives
1 fork with wooden handle
1 silver shaker
1 intact olive jar
1 silver spoon
1 brass knob
3 pieces copper sheathing, one with arrow
1 lead sinker

Cocoa frother—San Jose

Grinding *metate*

2 square bottom bottle bases
1 silver medallion
1 gold two escudo coin
1 square lead box
1 pewter dish
5 pewter plates
1 silver pendant
1 copper plate
3 *manos* (corn grinders)
1 section bronze blunderbuss
1 onyx bowl
7 pieces human skull bone
7 fishing leads
1 silver spur
1 woven cartridge belt
1 brass compass
114 broken pieces of
  Kang Hsi porcelain
1 broken container shot
5 clusters of cannon balls
94 cannon balls
30 bar shot
565 mini-balls (musket shot)
27 pieces of *manos* (corn grinders)
2 flintlock pistols
1 pair scissors
1 pair navigational dividers
2 pewter trays
2 black onion bottles
2 pottery jars
1 intact *Kang Hsi* porcelain cup
6 brass buttons

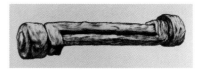

Bar-Shot

San Jose *Onion Bottle*

1 silver button
15 iron sailors palms
2 pieces broken comb
1 lock, hasp, and lock plate
1 brass hinge
2 small lead containers

Section of bronze blunderbuss—San Jose

3 bayonets
1 broken spoon handle
161 pieces of broken pottery shards
31 pieces lead sheet rolled around a rope
35 pieces of broken bottles
2 pieces lead pipe
9 pieces of square lead patches
1 piece lead pipe flanged on both ends
1 sheet of brass
1 large box of sailor's palms, iron
1 round lead container with square ends, one end with holes
2 pottery jars
2 single block with hook
2 large dead-eyes
1 double block
23 wooden sheaves
11 small pottery containers

Grifon Recoveries on **San Jose** - 1970
1 pair brass navigational dividers
2 silver buckles
15 musket balls
1 pottery bowl, intact
1 candelabra
3 keys
1 dress sword
12 silver coins
3 pewter plates
1 majolica plate, intact
1 silver fork with
   wooden handle
2 tear drop type locks
3 bayonets
1 sailor's palm
1 silver ring
1 silver bowl
2 silver medallions
1 silver knob

San Jose—*Candelabra*

1 silver ink well
2 pair scissors
1 glazed bellarmine stone jug
2 wooden sheaves
1 lifting cargo hook
1 pewter case or box
1 wooden block
2 pieces green slate
26 pieces of bellarmine
   stone ware
1 shaving tray
1 metal thumb screw

Encrusted axe head–Jose

Capitana Recoveries on **San Jose** - 1972
3 gold rings with emerald stones
6 gold ornate rings
10 religious medallions
3 flintlock pistols with
   ornate butt plates
2 gold buttons
2 gold brooches
1 ornate gold dinner bell
2 brass coin weights
3 large pewter serving trays
1 stack of silver plates
5 swords
17 buckles
1 ornate snuff box
1 complete ornate silver serving set
2 intact pottery olive jars
1 round snuff box
1 axe head
2 pewter porringers, ornate
1 sugar bowl with lid, silver
1 silver ink and shaker
approximately 250 pillar dollars 1732
several clumps of silver coins
miscellaneous. keys, scissors, locks,
   cannon balls, and other artifacts

Pillar Dollars

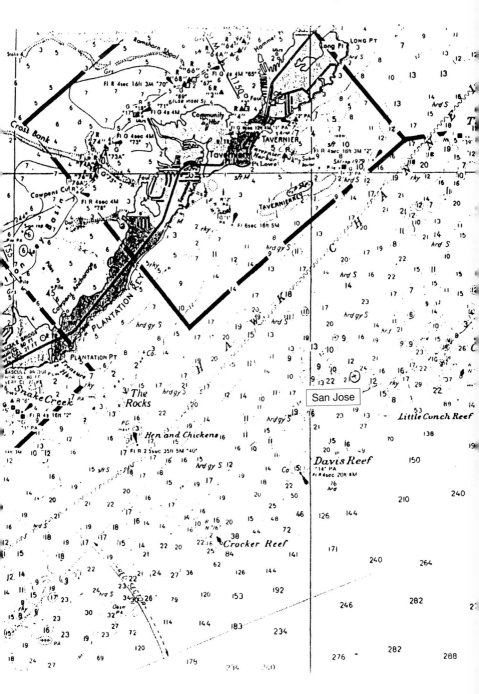

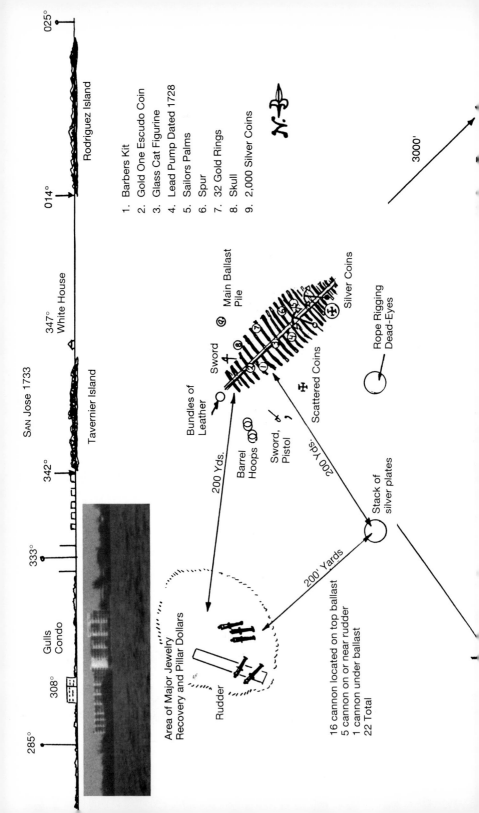

SAN JOSE 1733

285°   308°   333°   342°   347°   014°   025°
       Gulls   White House
       Condo   Rodriguez Island

Tavernier Island

1. Barbers Kit
2. Gold One Escudo Coin
3. Glass Cat Figurine
4. Lead Pump Dated 1728
5. Sailors Palms
6. Spur
7. 32 Gold Rings
8. Skull
9. 2,000 Silver Coins

Main Ballast Pile

Sword

Bundles of Leather

Barrel Hoops

Sword, Pistol

Scattered Coins

Silver Coins

Rope Rigging Dead-Eyes

Stack of silver plates

Area of Major Jewelry Recovery and Pillar Dollars

Rudder

200 Yds.

200 Yds.

200' Yards

16 cannon located on top ballast
5 cannon on or near rudder
1 cannon under ballast
22 Total

3000'

Salvage crew of the San Jose. Henry Taylor, Chuck Mitchell, Tom Gurr, George Hosford, Jim King. Photo Credit: Bob. Weller

Pewter plate, bone handle knives and spoon — San Jose

"Porcelain ginger jar" — San Jose

Artist Peter Copeland sketching artifacts underwater — San Jose

Engraving in wood — San Jose

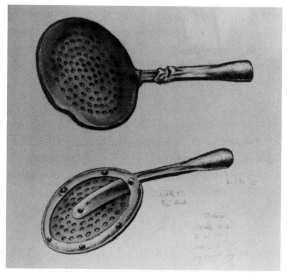

Cooking utensils — San Jose

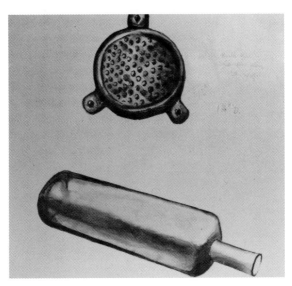

Iron sailors Palm and glass medicine bottle —
San Jose

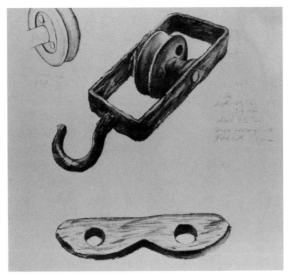

Cargo hook and roller — San Jose

3 gold coins recovered by the author from the Spanish plate fleet.
Photo Credit: E. Richards

"Pillar Dollar." Photo Credit: E. Richards

"Silver spur recovered from the San Jose.*"* Photo Credit: E. Richards

"Sand shaker, used to dry ink, 1733 Spanish Plate Fleet." Photo Credit: E. Richards

Gold ring embodied in coral, recovered from the Populo.
Photo Credit: E. Richards

*Two piles of ballast remains of the Navy schooner Alligator. Photo
Credit: Mike Richter*

The cannon on the San Jose

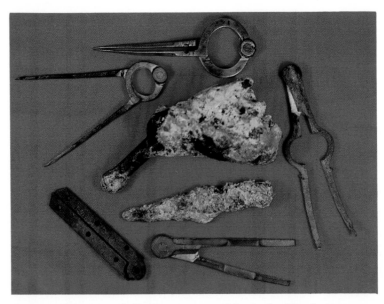

Bronze navigational dividers recovered from the Winchester. *Photo Credit: E.Richards*

Bone handled knives and brass navigational dividers recovered from the Winchester. *Photo Credit: E. Richards.*

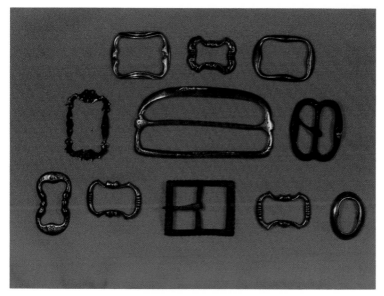

Brass buckles recovered from the Winchester. *Photo Credit: E. Richards*

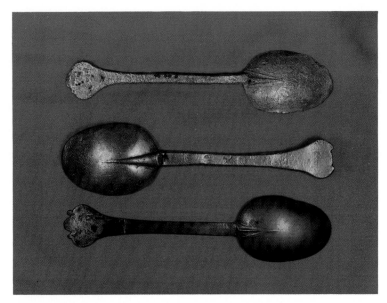

Brass and pewter spoons recovered from the Winchester. Photo Credit:
E. Richards

Tom Gurr and artifacts recovered from the San Jose.

Diver Don Kree with a 3 stone amethyst gold ring recovered from a Spanish galleon. Photo Credit: Jon Wilson

The author's salvage boat "Pandion". Photo Credit: Bob Weller

Diver handing up an encrusted sword from the San Jose.

Margaret Weller with a gold 4 Escudo "Royal" just recovered from a Spanish galleon.

Divers Steve Singer and author Bob Weller with 2 gold coins they recovered from a spanish galleon.

The "A" team. Steve Singer, Don Kree, Bob Luyendyk. Seated: Margaret Weller, Author - Bob Weller.

"Rings of the Spanish treasure fleet." Photo Credit: E. Richards

"Gold coins of the Spanish treasure fleet." Photo Credit: E. Richards

Sounding lead, recovered from the 1733 Spanish Plate Fleet." Photo
Credit: E. Richards

*"Ominous water spout a few hundred yards from salvage boat
"Pandion."*

Margaret Weller taking sextant readings.

Pewter money bag seals recovered from the 1733 Spanish Plate Fleet. Photo Credit: E. Richards

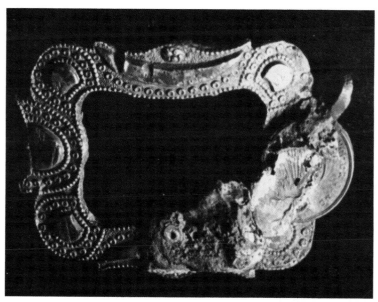

"Brass buckle with coral encrustation. 1733 Spanish Fleet."

Gold and silver coins, rings, gold bar, and a Kang Hsi bowl, recovered from the Spanish Plate Fleet, sunk on the Florida reefs.

Part of a Kang Hsi porcelain cup attached to an encrusted spike. Spanish Plate Fleet.

Jack Haskins raising the "Angustias" *cannon.*

Close-up of a 16' shark. Note Ramora just ahead of dorsal fin.

Sharks in a feeding frenzy. "Time to get out of the water!"

Ivory pocket sundial.

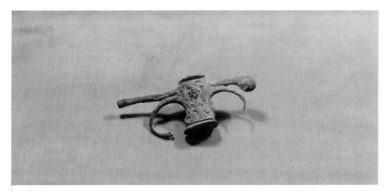

Silver dagger handle.

Engraved silver sword guard, recovered from the Spanish Plate Fleet. Photo Credits: E. Richards

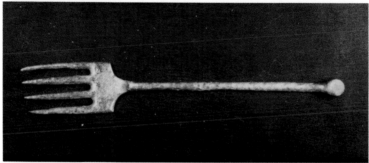

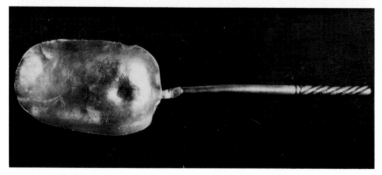

Padlock, silver fork and spoon. Recovered from the 1733 Spanish Plate Fleet. Photo Credits: E. Richards

Underwater on the ballast pile of "Alligator." *Photo Credits: E. Richards*

Chapter IV
The Buccaneers and the Alligator

Loran: 14086.8, 43305.7
Latitude: 24° 51.09'H
Longitude: 80° 37.08W'

At one time in history, over 10,000 bloodthirsty buccaneers roamed the coast and Keys of Florida and the Caribbean. It took a dedicated commodore, a young naval hero, and the *Alligator* to run them off. This is the story of the *Alligator*—a famous schooner pressed into service by the U.S. Navy—and its part in Florida history.

In the early 1800's, the Spanish colonies began a struggle for independence. They had seen the heyday of the Spanish Empire, but now the twilight had fallen on the once great caravans of gold and silver shipped via the "freight trains of the sea" back to Cadiz. The days of cannon power had been replaced by swift East India Merchantmen, French and British privateers, and by the fastest growing influence in the New World, the United States. As the colonies revolted against their appointed commissioners and governors, Spain declared a blockade of their ports. These colonies, in turn, declared a blockade of all ports still loyal to Spain, and so a Mexican stand-off resulted. These were lush days for piracy!

Spanish pirates based in Cuba, and using the Florida Keys and Bahama Out Islands for rendezvous areas, began to prey on ships of all other nations, particularly the United States. Under the pretext of enforcing one blockade or another, the buccaneers boarded hundreds of ships. Crews and passengers were brutally tortured to gain information on valuables hidden aboard ship. Afterwards, they were hacked to death and fed to the sharks. Spain could not cope with the estimated 10,000 bloodthirsty thieves that infested the area surrounding the Bahama Channel. In fact, it had reached the point where cargos were being plundered in Havana harbor!

By 1819 the buccaneers were out of control. The American public and press put up a strong protest for the Navy to do something—even if it were wrong. The U.S. Government needed little prodding to take charge of the situation. The boldness in the plundering of ships around the tip of Florida was incredible, and it was holding up the development of the Louisiana Purchase by slowing trade through the port of New Orleans. So it wasn't alligator hides nor a swamp-full of mosquitoes that forced the Congress to finally appropriate money for an expedition to rout the raiders. Command of a fleet of ships was given to an able and determined relative of the author, Commodore David Porter. Soon after Florida became a U.S. Territory, David was directed to Key West (then called Thompson's Island after the Secretary of the Navy) to establish a naval base of operation. From that point on he ran the pirates ragged. Constant patrols were set up on both the east and west coasts of Florida, across the Bahama Channel, and into the Caribbean. Porter's patrols were known to have chased some of the buccaneers into shallow waters where they abandoned their small craft and fled on foot into the mangroves. The boats were burned or were towed back to Thompson's Island. When the buccaneers were caught they were publicly executed . . . and sometimes not so publicly.

One of the most famous ships under Commodore Porter's command was the schooner *Alligator*. She was the third U.S. Naval warship to be named *Alligator*, this one constructed in the Boston Navy yard and launched on 2 November 1820. A 12 gun warship of 177 tons, 86 feet in length and $24^{1}/_{2}$ feet across the beam, she was fast and ideally suited for duty against the Barbary Coast and Caribbean pirates. The pirates used fast light schooners to overtake and outsail their victims. It took naval vessels with the swiftness and firepower of the *Alligator* to put an end to piracy on the high seas.

Her first Commanding Officer, Lieutenant Stockton, was more visionary than most. He persuaded the Secretary of the Navy, Smith Thompson, to give him his command in order to search for and acquire a stretch of the coast of Africa for the American Colonization Society. This Society had previously established a colony of former American slaves on the coast, but the climate in that particular area was unhealthy and as a result the colony eventually disintegrated. The Society had approached Stockton personally to aid them in looking for, and acquiring, a better parcel of land that a community of former slaves might survive on. When Stockton was given the first command of *Alligator,* he sailed for New York where he completed his crew, and Dr. Ayres, of the American Colonization Society came on board as an advisor. The *Alligator* was ready for her first cruise.

The *Alligator's* first orders were to cruise off the coast of Africa on a picket line from Cape Verde south to the Equator, on the lookout for slave ships *en route* from Africa to the Americas. The practice of slave trading in the early 1800's was as much a concern to the U.S. Navy as the activities of the Barbary Coast pirates. Slave trading was illegal in the Americas and the Navy had been put in the forefront of the fight to end the practice. As quickly as she arrived "on station" she swung into action, capturing the slave schooners *Mathilde,* *L'Eliza,* and *Daphne.* Word soon spread along the Ivory Coast that a fast new American warship was to be reckoned with. Slavers took other, longer routes, and sailed after dark to avoid the *Alligator.* But history was about to be made in a completely new arena.

Along the African coast was an area of good climate and fertile land, an area that Dr. Ayres felt was more suitable for colonization. The area was around Cape Mesurado, an area controlled by a native chieftain named King Peter. The problem facing Dr. Ayres and Lieutenant Stockton was that King Peter and his people were noted slavers themselves, warring against neighborhood tribes, and selling captives to the slave traders that frequented the coast. Initial negotiations between Ayres and the Chief seemed to go well, but as the treaty was about to be concluded something happened. The Chief left the coast and marched inland some 20 miles with his closest advisors, leaving Ayres and Stockton with a challenge to "follow him if they dare!" Although Stockton felt that this could be a trap, he accepted the challenge and literally the chase was on. The chase took them through swamps and jungles infested with the wildest animals this young Naval Lieutenant had ever seen. Fighting heat, insect bites, and even more hostile natives than the ones they were chasing, he finally succeeded in reaching the inland camp of King Peter. So surprised was the Chief and some 500 savage followers of his, that they ultimately agreed to the treaty. There was great relief and rejoicing on board *Alligator* when Ayres and Stockton returned safely. The result of their efforts was the beginning of—the Republic of Liberia.

The conclusion of the treaty completed the *Alligator's* first mission and she sailed for Boston harbor, arriving there in July, 1821. After several months of refitting she was ready for her next assignment, which again was stopping the slavers along the African coast. Leaving Boston on October 4 she arrived on station about three weeks later. Just as she began to settle into a routine, a strange sail was sighted on the horizon sailing on a course perpendicular to *Alligators*. On sighting the American warship, the stranger reduced sail and seemed to await her approach. Lookouts high in the crow's nest shouted down to Lt. Stockton that they could see a distress flag flying at the yardarm, so Stockton ordered his ship to sail towards the other ship to offer assistance. Suddenly, as *Alligator* moved within gun range, the stranger sprang to life and false gunports were pulled posing larger cannon than were carried by *Alligator*. Several puffs of smoke and the roar of cannon broke the silence that had separated the two vessels. Stockton ordered his men to lie flat on the deck after they had loaded their cannon, and he began to steer a zig-zag course that would bring his own cannon within range. The stranger hoisted a Portuguese flag and fired broadside after broadside at the American ship, wounding several of the crew of *Alligator* and causing some hull damage. The wind was slight that day and it was several hours before Stockton had his ship in position where he could fire. His men were ordered to station and the first broadside sent the deck hands of the other ship scurrying for cover. The cannon crews were well trained, and after 20 minutes of pouring broadsides into the enemy vessel and clearing her decks completely the enemy struck her colors. Stockton brought his ship alongside and hailed her, and soon her Captain appeared on deck. He claimed her to be a Portuguese Letter of Marque, but sailing under slightly different names. The one on her stern *Marianno Faliero*, and the one on her orders *Maraianna Flora*, led Stockton to believe they were pirates, and putting a prize crew aboard, sent her back to the United States to be condemned by an Admiralty Court. Years later the Portuguese Government requested and received the return of the vessel, but not before considerable political explanation and negotiations. The next several months went well for *Alligator* and a number of slavers were captured before her second cruise ended.

In was in the spring of 1822 that *Alligator* went through a change of command, and a change in her mission. Lieutenant William Allen became the new Commanding Officer, and she was assigned to Commodore Porter's fleet of naval warships operating out of Key West. To end the reign of piracy in the Caribbean was the mission. It was an enormous undertaking because the pirates knew the small islands and reefs firsthand, and their boats were usually fast and of shallow draft. Catching them was like catching a will-o-the-wisp. By April *Alligator* was on station off the coast of Cuba near the town of Nuevitas. A pirate schooner about the same size as *Alligator* was spotted close to shore and after several hours of dodging reefs the pirate vessel *Cienega* was captured and a prize crew put aboard.

The patrol of the *Alligator* took her along the northeast coast of Cuba in the Old Bahama Channel from Cay Sal to Punta Maisi. It was a dangerous channel to operate in, not more than a few miles wide in some areas, and near Cayo Romano the reefs were everywhere, as were the pirate vessels. Ships sailed this channel only because it offered the shortest route from Hispaniola and Puerto Rico to the ports of Havana and Nassau, as well as the entire east coast of Florida. In November Lieutenant Allen received word an American schooner and brig had been taken by a group of pirates. Fortunately the pirates spared the lives of the master and mate of the schooner, putting them ashore where they were later rescued. Allen brought the survivors on board his vessel and gave chase. He learned that the pirates were about 45 miles east of Matanza, in the vicinity of Bahia de Santa Clara, an area of many small islands and reefs. At dawn on November 9th he spotted the pirates, but by now the group had swelled to include five schooners, two brigs, and another larger ship. It seemed *Alligator* was seriously out-gunned, and certainly out-manned. The nearest help was Havana harbor over 100 miles to the west. Allen felt that if he could sail into the group and cause sufficient confusion he could recapture one or more of the ships. But winds are fickle, as the sun came up, the winds died down. Not a puff of wind, neither land breeze nor sea breeze, filled the air. The adversaries stood facing each other with a mile of open, flat calm water between. It was a Mexican stand-off, but not for long. The intrepid naval lieutenant ordered his executive officer Lieutenant John Dale, to take charge of the *Alligator* while he lowered all his longboats, filled them with eager sailors armed with rifles and boarding swords, and began rowing toward the becalmed pirate vessels. The ship closest to them was a heavily armed schooner with at least five cannon on board. As the longboats approached, the schooner opened fire with cannon and small arms fire, and although none of the cannon balls found their mark, it was a precarious situation. Allen pressed the attack and soon brought his longboats alongside the schooner. A fierce, sharp battle took place on the main deck during which Lieutenant Allen was mortally wounded by two musket balls. The schooner was captured, but the death of their Captain so incensed the *Alligator* crew they rowed from one ship to the other capturing them all except a single schooner that managed to catch a wisp of breeze and disappear behind the nearby islands.

With all the pirate vessels in convoy and a prize crew aboard each ship, the *Alligator* headed for the coast of Florida. Just before dawn on the following day, as the ships approached the hazardous reefs five miles off the Florida Keys, a stiff breeze came up driving the *Alligator* onto the reef that now bears her name. The ship struck hard, and although Dale and his crew worked desperately to refloat their ship it was hopeless. Four days kedging anchors and deballasting proved fruitless. On 23 November, 1822 they set fire to their proud ship, and the young but battle-tested warship soon blew up.

The story of the *Alligator* gained national attention, and Thompson's Island was renamed "Allentown." "Allen" became the war cry in many later battles, and the pirates were ultimately driven from the waters around Cuba and the Bahamas. Allentown was later renamed "Key West." A powerful beam of light atop a 110 foot tower stands sentinel on Alligator Reef, warning ships to stand clear, and keeping a watchful eye on the small ballast pile that lies on the finger of reef stretching to the south and seaward.

The Earliest Known Sketch of Key West done by Titian R. Peale in 1826 shows settlement that Commodore David Porter called Allentown.

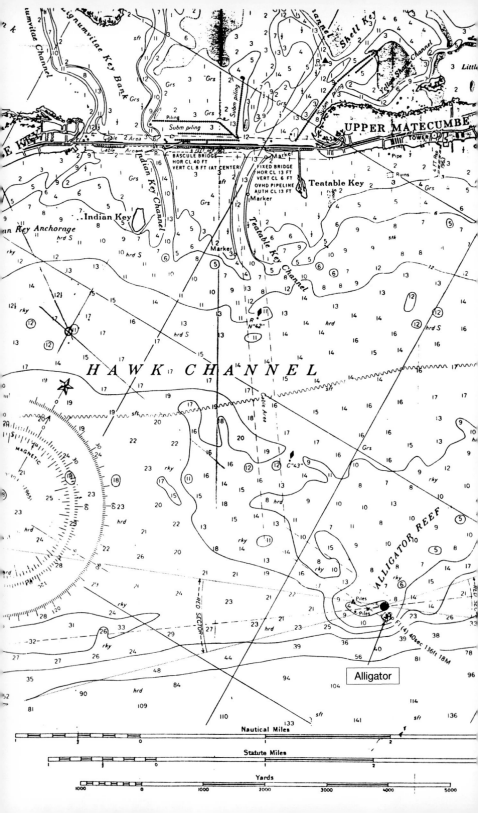

Note Position
of Boarding Platform
on Shoreward Side of Light

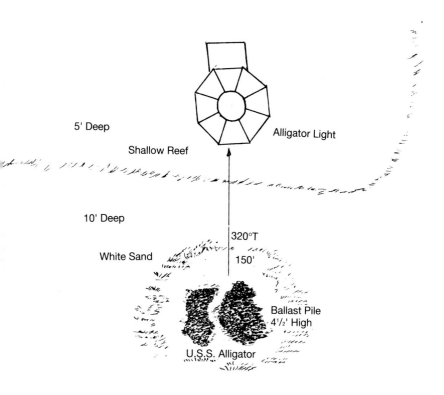

5' Deep

Shallow Reef

Alligator Light

10' Deep

White Sand

320°T

150'

Ballast Pile
4¹/₂' High

U.S.S. Alligator

Chapter V
Angustias 1733

Alias: Nuestra Señora de Las
  Angustias, el Charanguero
  Grande, San Rafael
Loran: 14057.17, 62406.70
Latitude: 24° 47' 27" N
Longitude: 80° 51' 52" W

Every once in a while a true treasure story involving research and common sense comes down the pipeline, proving the point that anyone with the enthusiasm and desire to follow their instincts can find the end of the rainbow. The *Angustias* is that kind of a story. The story involves a poem, of all things, and two serious treasure divers from the Florida Keys that believe in doing their "homework." Written in flowery prose by one of the survivors of the treasure galleon *Angustias*, the key to treasure lay within the poem, a key that all other salvage divers had missed.

> "On those of a stoney reef she stumbled
> impelled, and almost hit a reef, and in
> her death throes our tormented ship was
> caught by that great iron ring, which
> chain of strong flint was seriously shaken
> until the side was dented with rage, and
> such fury that the valiant keel broke."

The 60 page poem written in prose in 1734 by Don Jose Ignacio de Toca Velasco and printed in Madrid under the title "Triaca Producida de un Veneno" described the sailing of the Spanish treasure fleet from Havana and the destruction of the fleet as a hurricane drove the frail ships onto the Florida reefs. Jose was a passenger on the treasure *nao Nuestra Señora de las Angustias*.

On July 13, 1733 the treasure fleet of 21 ships set sail from Havana with their final destination the home port of Cadiz, Spain. In their holds they carried 20,000,000 *pesos* of silver and gold, the results of several years of mining and minting coinage in the New Spain, now Mexico. The sailing had been delayed for several months due to ship's repairs, provisioning, and parties in the "Emerald of the Caribbean" . . . the port of Havana. The fleet was finally able to weigh anchor and sailed on a southeasterly breeze for the Bahama Channel.

"With such a pretty day the thirteenth day of July of this year the fleet stubbornly weighed anchor. The foretopsail was run up and they sailed with the gentle tide. At the push of the great task, to send itself wind, it was born off. So from the Gran Philipo, the great fleet with generous south easterlies set sail. And coming on bearing the course was picked up, a line of foam parallel. The broken mouth of Havana harbor strangled between such mountains appeared wind, which helped."

Unknown to the General of the Fleet Rodrigo de Torres y Morales, a hurricane was already in full force less than 500 miles away and bearing down rapidly on the Bahama Channel. Two days from Havana the seas became listless and the skies took on an ominous hue of an impending storm. The old seaman's saying "Red skies in the morning . . . sailor take warning. Red skies at night . . . sailors delight" was enough to cause the General of the Fleet to make a course change that would take them back to Havana. But, it was too late—the hurricane was upon them.

"With a thousand gifts, 40 hours and 30 leagues, they saw her pilgrim. The advance was not great because over-coming risks

were present, already shown in the sky which
appeared as a diamond tiara. It was 2 A.M.
Tuesday night when the storm broke. So in
the torn dark mouth of the Bahama channel,
with yawning to swallows wants the same it
provokes, in seething caldrons its raging
torrents, in whose horrible gloomy shadows
I will relate the torment of my Angustias."

The *Angustias* was stationed near the center of the fleet,
and not being a large merchant ship it carried only four cannon and not a great deal of treasure. The owner and captain of
the ship was D. Francisco Sanchez Madrid a seasoned ship-
master, but his ship was no match for the towering 20 foot
waves.

"Flee afflicted, but from whom do you run
if the violent hurricane stays with you.
Very well the region, whips the wing, swells
the water, the waves crash and the tempest
increases as hell breaks loose. The
whirlwind continues in gusts to cruelly
buffet the foretopsail, and its topgallant
the topmosts and the sharp pine bows and
the yard snaps and the mast sail and yard
become entangled in a fatal forelock. When
the broken sail is taken down and prompt
repair vacillates by inept practice, finally
the mist takes the sail.
Thus died her hope, thus ended, now the helm
governs no longer and at the mercy of the
wind she turns without steerage or lantern
or compass. So the vessel receives squint -
eyed the blows sending in balance the strong
blows of the sea.
From the sharp axes the stakes break tackle
and the main and mizzen must fall into the

sea. The ship saw the silver reef, resting
abject in the sea which Nereus dilated.
There was only time to sigh, to ask for
grace. Clouds and waves in approaching
mountains make her boards sad horizons. The
great hold which groaned cluttered, cries
insatiable for water, afflicted."

Many of the passengers and crew of the *Angustias* lost their
lives, but the author Velasco was one of those fortunate
enough to float ashore near what is today known as Long Key.
Of the twenty-one ships of the Torres fleet, only one remained
afloat when the hurricane passed. The other ships were scattered along the reefs and shallows of the Florida Keys from
Largo to Marathon.

Eventually at least three more merchant ships were refloated and returned to Spain. For years historians, and salvagers,
held the opinion that the *Angustias* was also refloated and
returned to Spain. Although a common name, a ship named
Angustias passed over the bar at Cadiz in 1734. Of the ships
that were known to have swamped and sunk on the reefs,
treasure divers have systematically located and salvaged their
remains. From the ballast piles of the *El Infante, San Jose, El
Capitana, Herrera, Tres Puentes, San Pedro, San Fernando,
Arizon, El Populo,* and *San Francisco* some of the greatest
Spanish artifacts had been recovered.

By the winter of 1971 most the television and newspaper
media had shifted their attention 200 miles north where the
1715 fleet recoveries were big news. Here gold and silver were
coming up off the bottom daily from sites between Sebastian
inlet and Ft. Pierce along the east coast of Florida. All seemed
quiet in the Florida Keys, except for two diligent divers intent
on doing their homework. Jack Haskins and Richard
MacAllaster were on the trail of *Angustias*. The ship had a
nickname *Charanguero Grande* or Grand Coastal Trader.
Although there was a similarity of ships' names returning to
Cadiz in 1734 something nagged at Haskins and MacAllaster.

In the poem written by Velasco the one passage "Until the side was dented with rage, and such fury that the valiant keel broke," seemed to stand out. Haskins' literal interpretation of this passage was that at first the *Angustias* was held from smashing onto the reefs by the anchor. But when the huge waves smashed in her side and finally broke her keel. . . "When the keel breaks you can be sure that ship was never salvaged!" Haskins pointed out. "So it has to be right there where the old maps placed it." Jack was to make at least five trips to the *Archivos de Las Indias* in Seville, Spain. On the first trip he had less than a dozen words of Spanish in his vocabulary, and a Spanish dictionary. By the time he made his fifth trip he could read archaic Spanish fluently.

There were six different maps of the location of Torres shipwrecked fleet, each with a variation in ships names and locations. On the last trip Jack felt he had positive identification, and location, of the *Angustias*. The next step was for MacAllaster to make a trip to Tallahassee where he applied to the State Bureau of Historic Sites and Properties, Division of Archives History and Records Management for an exploration contract. By September 18, 1972 the State granted an exploration contract to "Peninsular Exploration and Salvage Co." the joint venture that Haskins and MacAllaster were to operate under. Financial backing came from a local Marathon resident Rex deRosay. They were ready and eager to go.

Jack Haskins owned a 38' Mathews converted charter boat named *Trident,* and with another local diver Jim Jones, they left the Toll Gate Inn dockage at upper Matecumbe for the search area 15 miles further down the keys. As the boat rounded the sand bars that mark the seaward end of the Teatable Key channel the *Trident* developed engine trouble. The transmission filled with water throwing oil and water all over the engine compartment. After drifting around for a while the two divers managed to get the engine going again, and rather than limp back to their dock decided to go on with the search. Within an hour they were in the search area, bounded by Long Key on the north, Duck Key to the west, the overseas bridge and U.S. Highway #1 linking the two keys, and the open seas to the south. The grid they laid out with bright colored buoys was about one square mile in area. Selecting their initial search path they strung out a magnetometer, that electronic fish that is towed behind the boat to detect metal on the ocean bottom, and headed into the swift moving water of Long Key channel that marked their first run.

U.S. Highway #1 skips along the Florida Keys connecting the mainland at Florida City to Key West some 130 miles to the west in a curving scimitar. Many years ago Henry Flagler built a railroad tying the mainland to the sleepy shrimp-port of Key West. It opened the emerald islets to the tourists that flocked to this sun-filled vacation of clear water and deep sea fishing. The railroad vanished in the 200 mile an hour winds and mountainous waves of the 1935 hurricane that swept across the keys, destroying most everything it its path. Debris from this hurricane remains today, railroad ties and rails, spikes, destroyed homes, still lie buried in the sand and reefs in the nearshore area of each key where the railroad was to be. As the years passed, and it became established along the keys, the overseas highway was built. Reinforced concrete and many steel columns were used in the construction to brace against the future onslaught of high winds. It was a major engineering feat when it was completed.

As Jack Haskins navigated his boat into the swift current near the overseas bridge he had to be careful not to snag his magnetometer on the coral heads or uneven bottom that marked the edge of the channel. It was a clear day, and the water visibility was 30 feet or more. They could easily see the bottom of the channel nine feet deep as they neared the shadows of the bridge. Almost immediately the magnetometer began registering "hits" or anomalies that indicate metal on the bottom. Jack felt sure this was nothing more than construction "junk" or debris from the old 1935 hurricane. He was sure that some of it was metal lobster pots that seemed to be everywhere, and he steered the *Trident* in a zig-zag to keep from getting his prop fouled in the buoy lines. Actually the hits

were part of his missing *Angustias,* but Jack would not know
that until later. On their fourth run along the grid pattern they
suddenly got a very large anomaly. "It was so big that when I
asked Jimmy to drop a buoy on the hit, he asked what part of
the hit?" Looking down at the bottom of the channel they
could see the ring at the end of a large anchor, and then the
ballast pile. It had taken less than four hours from dockside to
tying the marker buoy to one of the giant anchors. The *Angustias* had been found!

In the weeks that followed the request was granted by the
State of Florida for Peninsular Salvage to dig an exploratory
trench and two test holes in the ballast to help positively identify the ship. Anchors sometimes help, and there were four
huge ones lying on the seaward end of the ballast mound. Two
cannon were lying off to one side, and another was later found
about 90 feet to seaward. These did indicate the wreck-site
was about the right time period, but more proof was needed
before the group could commit itself to many, many diving
hours on the bottom in a salvage operation. The first test hole
near the bow produced nothing to indicate the ship's identification. The second test hole in the edge of the ballast nearest
the bridge which they felt was the stern section, produced a
number of rosary beads and some pottery shards. This left
only a test trench which they decided to make near the stern
section. Halfway across the ballast pile they got their answer!
A single gold coin, a two escudo minted in Mexico, not quite
the size of a nickel, but unmistakably 1724-27 and in excellent
condition. Excitement and emotions were certainly in order
for this jubilant group of divers.

A salvage contract was issued by the State in December, too
late for diving on the site because even in Florida cold weather
brings poor visibility to the Keys. In the swift and murky
waters of Long Key channel it was imperative that the divers
have decent visibility underwater. So salvage operations were
planned for the following spring . . . and it was a long winter
to sit out. The single coin brought visions of a pot of gold at
the end of the rainbow over the Long Key Bridge. Many days

were spent driving back and forth over the bridge, or just standing at the edge of Long Key and gazing at the changing tides. But it gave them a chance to locate a larger salvage vessel and plan the systematic search of not only the ballast area, but the area inshore towards the bridge and seaward where the channel merges into Hawks Channel. Don George had been involved in the Padre Island salvage of the 1553 Spanish Plate Fleet, and was a co-owner of the 60 foot salvage vessel *Geo-Search*. He joined the operation with enthusiasm, and by the spring of 1973 the equipment and divers were ready.

The ballast mound was 95' long by 35' wide, and about four feet high. It represented about 400 tons of smooth river rock that had to be moved by hand. Much of the ballast was welded together by iron fittings that had become part of the pile.

In addition, the strong current and sometimes murky visibility of muddy sand flowing out of the Gulf of Mexico side of the bridge provided problems that had to be dealt with. An inner tube was strung out on a 100 foot tether behind the *Geo-Search*. Instructions to all the divers were, work near the boarding ladder, so that when you head for the surface you're not swept out of reach. If you miss the ladder, and the inner tube, just let the current take you out of the channel a mile or so . . . swim over to Long Key. Then walk along the Overseas Highway Bridge until you're opposite the boat, jump over the side of the bridge and let the current bring you back for another pass." No one ever missed the inner tube. Another unseen danger were the sharks. The channels are a favorite feeding ground for all kinds of sharks, and the *Angustias*, with the myriads of bait fish that called the wreck their home, was a natural attraction for large hungry fish. In the weeks that followed the divers would see enough marine life to last a lifetime. The first few weeks of hard work seemed to sing out "Treasure - Treasure." First a silver dinner bell, then a complete *Kang Hsi* porcelain cup . . . unusual in itself to remain unbroken under the ballast pile, silver plated rosary beads, a jade Buddah, and then one of the divers came up the boarding ladder with a pewter jewel box under each arm. You can imagine the anticipation as they were carefully opened and the contents of rosary beads spread out on deck. The greatest excitement came when what appeared to be a rectangular box 20"x16"x9" and weighing 236.6 pounds came up off the bottom. That's about the right weight for a box of silver Pieces of Eight, about 3,000 to be exact. The box was sent up to the Department of Archives in Tallahassee for preservation. Greyhound bus drivers were heard directing the attention of their passengers to the "Treasure salvage boat anchored on the left, bringing up gold doubloons and pieces of eight from the remains of an old Spanish shipwreck." The highway was only 1500 feet away and I am sure the southbound passengers were treated to some diver Irish jigs on the fantail as the artifacts began to fill all the water-filled containers around the stern of the *Geo-Search*.

Near the area of the jewel boxes a great many pewter crosses were recovered, obviously part of the cargo. Also, a silver locket with a glass bezel and what appeared to be a painting on the inside. As the ballast stones were removed from the stern section another cannon was uncovered. Jimmy Jones had been chipping away at what he described as a "pretty big cannon ball near the bottom of the ballast pile," when MacAllaster pointed out that it was the cascabel of a cannon. He had uncovered the muzzle on the other side of the pile! Don George recovered a beautiful silver buckle near the bow section, but suddenly the artifacts seemed to dry up. Here and there a button or a few musket balls, but nothing really exciting. It was about this time that the divers began to notice the fish, and there were a lot of them. They crowded around the airlift and waited for a free meal, the sea worms that are sucked up the tube. As soon as one would disappear up the tube there would be a flurry of fish to the top of the tube, and as it emerged a fight would take place with the largest fish dashing off with the worm in its mouth, and the others in hot pursuit. The author, Bob Weller, heard a rubbing sound while working near the bow. It resembled a ship rubbing up against some rubber tire pilings at dockside. He soon found the source of the noise when he noticed a 400 pound jewfish with his head inside one of the large anchor rings about 10 feet away. rubbing his back scales against the inside of the upright anchor ring, not unlike an itching horse and an old fence post. The jewfish was part of the local scenery, and after he had moved off to his favorite hole under the timbers, a survey of the ring indicated he had used this scratching post for years. Bernie Smith made the mistake of opening a few scallops for a five pound sheepshead that had been watching his every move. A scallop slipped down the ballast pile a few feet away and Bernie didn't see it. The sheepshead began darting back and forth from the diver to the scallop. Finally the fish actually picked up the scallop in his mouth and swam over to where Bernie was working an airlift, spitting it out in front of him. He opened the shell for the fish, and the fish swam off, probably looking for more scallops. The day the big shadow passed over the wreck-site caused some consternation for the divers on the bottom. The divers topside saw the big shark and made a lot of surface noises, and it picked up speed on its way to seaward. The ballast, like other shipwreck piles, are full of eels. The *Angustias* pile was no different, some of the eels were thick as your arm and over five feet long. Each diver wore heavy rubber gloves, but they're no match for the razor sharp teeth of a moray. One day an eel followed MacAllaster along the bottom and up to the surface boarding ladder, curious about the contents of MacAllaster's "goodie" bag.

What seemed to be the final artifact was a three legged *metate* used for grinding corn or flour on board ship. After that nothing was found as the last of the ballast were turned over. Everyone tagged the wreck-site as "cleaned" and it was time to raise the cannon. The last job in any salvage operation is raising the cannon, and these were six foot beauties. As they were being raised, Jack Haskins was making a final inspection of all the little pot-holes around the perimeter of the ballast pile. Several yards towards the bridge he found a pot-hole about a foot in diameter that hadn't been cleaned out. As he fanned away the sand and coral his eyes became as big as saucers; the glint of gold does that to every red-blooded Vermonter. There, stuck to the bottom of the hole, was a beautiful round gold four escudo! After several moments of chipping away at the edges, he carried his prize to the surface with a "Yippee!" The coin proved to be a 1732 Royal, an extremely valuable coin that later auctioned at over $17,000. It was a suitable ending for a successful salvage operation.

The wreck-site is now abandoned to the fish characters who will miss us divers I am sure. We miss them as well, but we treasure the hours and days spent on the wreck-site, with the turn of each ballast stone promising a new reward. So long, *Angustias.*

Cannon on the Angustias *ballast pile.* Photo Credit - Mike Cassady

Angustias

Coral encrusted anchor ring — Angustias

The author working the ballast pile of Angustias.

A 10' shark swims over the ballast pile of Angustias.

"Iron Mike" the local Barracuda — Angustias

A rare gold 4 Escudo — dated 1732 — Angustias. *Photo Credit: Richard MacAllaster*

One of the 8' Angustias cannons being raised.

The author and Jack Haskins during Angustias *salvage.*

Haskins search boat "Trident" after locating the Angustias.

Chapter VI
Sueco de Arizón 1733

Alias: Nuestra Señora del
   Rosario, San Antonio,
   Y San Vicente Ferrer
Loran: 14053.0, 43380.3
Latitude: 24° 46'.38"m N.
Longitude: 80° 53;.56"m W.

This is the true story of the author's first treasure recovery. In 1966, while working the 1733 Spanish Plate Fleet wreck-sites, his group of week-end divers recovered a large number of silver coins on the Sueco de Arizón. *This is their story.*

I swam back to the stern of the boat. Brad Patten and Pat Patterson were pulling in one of the air hoses. It was late in the day, the water was rough, and we were ready to go in. I leaned over the stern and said, "Boys, we've hit it! We've really hit it! The bottom's covered with silver!" The reaction was instantaneous. Brad and Pat piled over the side and headed for the bottom to see for themselves. It didn't matter that they both forgot face masks and fins. Treasure does that to you.

We had been working the wreck of the *Arizón*, a Spanish galleon that sank near Duck Key in the Florida Keys July 15, 1733. Later, after we had filled three plastic, five gallon buckets with coins, I remember standing on the stern. Suddenly I cut loose with a yell people must have heard a thousand yards away on shore. I shouted something like "Ai-Yi-Yi-Yip-Pahoo!" Then I did a jig on the stern. After all the trouble, after all the agonizing disappointments, after all the work, after week-ends that seemed to stretch back endlessly, we'd finally hit it! I couldn't control myself! That's how it feels to find a sizeable amount of sunken treasure. You can't describe the experience adequately, of course, for the emotions are too intense. You become incoherent, and you do silly things—

such as counting the loot fifty times, caressing the coins and even hugging them like an idiot. You stutter. Maybe you start a sentence ten times and never remember to finish it. It isn't the money that's important—although our find was a sizeable amount, particularly for week-end divers. It's the victory that really steams you up. Let's not get literary about it, but Stevenson knew this when he wrote *Treasure Island*. Only a few lines are devoted to the actual treasure. The real story is the search, the frustrations, the exciting adventures, and the victory at the end knowing you beat the odds. And so it was with us. Our group "Royal Fifth," named after the King's *quinto* or tax on treasure from the New World, began on a warm summer evening on my pool patio in South Miami. A neighbor of mine, Pat Patterson, came up with an idea. He had been diving with me on my 16' Mohawk boat and had become an avid treasure bug like myself. He knew some money people in Chicago, and felt that if we put a prospectus together they might be willing to financially back us. We thought $8,000 would buy us the bigger boat we needed, along with replacing the worn-out equipment that would keep us on the bottom all day instead of fighting cranky Briggs and Stratton gas engines that ran our air compressor. We picked the name Royal Fifth and I wrote the propectus around the salvage of another 1733 galleon, the *El Infante*. I had recovered two gold rings and several dozen Pieces of Eight from her over the previous five years, and felt that under the turn of her hull timbers we could find gold. But to dig under the hull required better equipment than I presently owned.

It turned out that our financial backers came from an entirely unexpected source. My patio had standing water on it after a rain, and being less than a year old, the real estate agent that sold me the house came over to look at it. He happened to see my collection of shipwreck artifacts and mentioned he had two partners that would like to get into the treasure thing. Two other divers, Brad Patten and Ray Manieri, joined our group. A meeting was called to meet our prospective backers, Al, Norman, and Manuel. I can remember looking across my dinner table at these three excited, middle-aged men and asking, "Why do you want to throw your money away on a treasure diving project?" Silence was absolute, until finally Al Greenberg said, "Well Bob, we want to be a part of a real treasure diving operation. We want to get in your way, we want our kids on the boat, we want to take photos, we want to tell our grandchildren some day—we dug for treasure on an old Spanish galleon!" Before the evening was over we had our deal, enough to buy a good second-hand boat and proper equipment. As it turned out, Norman Sondberg was a lawyer, and had come to this meeting prepared to shoot me down. When I opened with my statement, as he said later, "It took all the wind out of my sails. I had no choice but to listen, and the more I listened the more I wanted to get started."

We bought a 32' former dive boat, *The Big Fisherman.* Twin gas engines, with a fly bridge and stern large enough to load all our gear and not trip over each other. I can remember my first run down Biscayne Bay on a flat calm day. There's a shoal at the south end called Mosquito Bank. You have to thread your way through a narrow channel, then out Black Caesar's Creek to open water. It was an untypical foggy Saturday morning, the boat was big—twice the size of my Mohawk, and unfamiliar. Somehow we got behind the bar at Mosquito Bank and grounded. We grounded again. Finally grounding once more in the process, we managed to get through Black Caesar's Creek into safe water - if you can call it that.

It was hilariously funny as each of us took turns steering from the flying bridge, weaving around coral heads that seemed to be just below the surface. It was funnier still when we reached Mandalay Boat Basin in Key Largo late that afternoon. We had a little old tin horn on board, and we nearly blew it to death as we were coming in. As a result a lot of people came down to the dock to watch us. About that time our starboard engine quit. With the wind from the wrong direction, I tried, and tried again to back the boat into the narrow slip that the dockmaster was pointing out to us. No soap. Finally an old lady threw us a line and we were sheepishly hauled in backwards to the pier and tied up. I don't know what happened to the tin horn after that. During the next three week-ends we outfitted the boat. We rigged four air-lift pipes on an aircraft A/C compressor, and a 6" water dredge on a $7^1/_2$ H.P. Hale fire pump. There were racks made for everything, and new fins and face masks for each diver. We were so excited during this period that we actually ran while doing errands. We seemed to feel that the treasure wouldn't wait another day for us, even though it had been lying on the bottom for 232 years. I can remember the first Sunday we took the *Big Fisherman* out on a trial run. We had all the backers, our wives and kids. Must have been over a dozen of us. We anchored in behind Rodriguez Island where there's a sandy bottom, the water is gin clear and only four feet deep. I sat up on the flying bridge watching everyone having fun. I really felt good.

We began working the *El Infante*. The work was slow and hard, with tons of ballast stone to be moved by hand. We tunnelled under the hull by the fourth week-end, and were disappointed. A single gold link to a money chain was our total reward. Somewhere in the ballast pile we had picked up a corroded silver "Piece of Four." Not much for our efforts, and at that point it didn't appear as though the treasure situation would improve. My hunch about the gold under the hull hadn't turned out.

Mel Fisher was making a modern day legend out of himself and his group Treasure Salvors, in the Ft. Pierce area. I knew Mel personally and decided to pay him a visit. He was living on Banyan Street in Vero Beach at the time, and after dinner we walked the beach behind the Driftwood Inn. I told him I had a good crew and the right equipment. If his group Armada Research, in Marathon down in the Florida Keys, had more wrecks than they could handle, give me a chance at one of them, I'd split 50-50. Mel has that trusting smile, and he turned it on me. "Go on down to Marathon and I'll call Dick Williams and let him know you're coming. He'll give you one of our wrecks. Let's see what you can do with it." The trip back to Miami that night was exhilarating. I felt we had a chance to find something, a chance to work a virgin wreck-site. Dick Williams met with us at Christensen's Motel in Marathon. He brought along Bobby Jordan to look us "week-enders" over. I assured Dick that if there was anything on the wreck-site he was about to give us—we'd find it! He pointed to a spot on the chart about 1000 yards NE of Duck Key, and about 400 yards from the tip of Walker's Island. "We've buoyed a wreck there with a cluster of red Clorox bottles. I think it's *Sueco de Arizón*, one of the 1733 Spanish Plate Fleet. It's all yours."

The Sueco had the usual Spanish name *Nuestra Señora del Rosario, San Antonio Y San Vicente Ferrer* and, it was not unusual to have the ship referred to as simply the "Ship of Captain . . . " In this case the Captain was Juan Jose de Arizón, and the owner was Jacinto de Arizón. This made it easier to call her *Sueco de Arizón*: or Swede of Arizon. When it sank it was carrying 24,000 pesos in silver specie and bullion, and a general cargo including tobacco, dyestuff, and leather. When the *Sueco* was driven through the reefs by the hurricane it managed to remain fairly intact until it reached the shallows near present day Duck Key. Here she began striking the tops of the reefs and her hold filled with water. She settled in nine feet of water, her bow to seaward, her stern pointed at the tip of Walker's Island. Mel had filed a State lease on the *Sueco*, along with 26 over wreck-sites Armada Research had located, and our salvage followed State regulations to the letter. We managed to berth the *Big Fisherman* behind the Indies House on Duck Key in exchange for publicity on our activities.

That first day on the wreck-site was unforgettable. Ray Manieri was first on the bottom and he checked the ballast pile over. "It's intact, doesn't look like anyone has worked it!" That first day we just spent checking the extent of scatter and laying out a grid pattern across the ballast that we could follow. We did recover shards of blue and white *Kang Hsi* porcelain, and parts of clay olive jars. Both indications that there was a good possibility the site was a Spanish shipwreck.

The following weekend we began methodically working the pile. The ballast stones were welded together by iron fittings and spikes. We drew sketches, took photographs, and finally began hammering apart the pile, rock by rock. The pile was initially 60' long by 20' wide and about 3^1/$_2$' high. By the fourth weekend, in fact July 4th weekend, we had narrowed the pile down to 15'; by 5', and so far hadn't found much to get excited about. Some cannon balls, musket balls, a couple of silver coins, and some pottery shards. Brad and Pat had already called it a day and were up in the boat relaxing. Ray and I were still hammering away at what was left of the pile. I had discovered what at first looked like a whole *Kang Hsi* porcelain cup welded to the bottom. As I gingerly picked at it I found it to be only half a cup. Still, a nice find, and I picked it up and headed for the surface. Ray, working just on the other side of the pile, came up with me. On the surface he said, "Bob, I've got five Pieces of Eight!" He had them in the pocket of a yellow pullover he was wearing, and suddenly it was as if lightning had struck. He said, "Tell the boys not to shut off our air!" and headed back for the bottom, while I headed for the stern of the *Big Fisherman.*

When I shouted "Boys, we've hit it!" pandemonium couldn't describe our actions. We had been looking a long time, and to suddenly find what we were looking for . . . the end of the rainbow right there under the boat! The entire 5 foot by 15 foot pile of ballast stone seemed to suddenly have coins sticking out from under it everywhere. They were embedded in coral, stuck to ballast stones, or stuck to the bottom. When we filled one plastic bucket full of coins one of us would take it to the surface and bring down another bucket. By the time he hit the bottom we would have a pile of coins waiting. It was getting dark, and we had milked the main fuel tank of gas to keep the air compressor going. We weren't sure we had enough gas to get back to the dock, and if one of us had to swim to shore for fuel we wanted to do it while there was still daylight. We could still see coins under the remaining ballast stones, we didn't know how much was still there, but we wanted to go slowly so we didn't miss anything. We hated to leave treasure on the bottom, but we did want to share this find with our backers. They had been just great, and they deserved to be a part of this find. So, we piled ballast stone around the edge of the remaining pile so that no one could spot the coins without tearing the rest of the pile apart, hauled in our anchors, and headed for the dock.

We had told our wives that if we ever hit it big, we would come in with our divers flag flying. Someone raised the flag as we rounded the breakwater heading into the Duck Key dockage. The girls were standing on the dock, but they didn't get the significance of the flag, but the plastic buckets full of coins did the trick! We had a lot of back-slapping and hugging on the dock. Pat suggested we call the backers and give them the good news. And a celebration was certainly in order. There was a phone booth down at the end of the dock, so we all headed for it. While Pat was making the call, I looked around . . and saw our boat drifting away from the dock! We had too much excitement around us to remember to even tie up the boat! I jumped in and swam out to get it, a little embarrassed.

By the time we loaded all our gear in the cars and drove the 90 miles back to Miami, the party was already in progress. Through several bottles of champagne and toasting, we made plans for the following weekend to rent several rooms at Christiansen's Motel and bring our families. I'm not sure how we made it through that following week. We had no idea how many coins were still on the bottom, and much of the time was spent on the phone finalizing plans and trying to count all the coins we already had in the three buckets. Our minds were certainly not on our jobs.

On Friday we piled into our cars—the backers and and everyone—and headed for the Keys. That night at Christiansens we planned the morning dive as carefully as we could. We were up most of the night, who could sleep . . . and at dawn we were on the wreck. Ray and I marked a large area around the ballast pile with ski rope to make sure we covered every crack or crevice where coins could be hiding. Then Ray, his son, Brad and I began working our way slowly over the bottom towards where we had piled ballast over the remaining coins. The backers were snorkeling on the surface, the wives and kids as well, watching us as we finally reached the pile and began taking the stones away. Before long we were piling up coins on the bottom, and Manuel Serkin's son swam the first bucket down for us to fill. One of the first things I spotted was two Pillar Dollars stuck together. This is a rare coin, the first round milled dollar ever made in the New World, and they were all lost on the 1733 fleet. These two were in mint condition; the date 1732 looked as if it had been minted yesterday. As the coins came up off the bottom everyone seemed to be caught up in the excitement. Each one in turn was holding his breath and coming down for a look. It was great.

By noontime we had moved the last ballast stone and had picked up the last coin. It was a tired happy bunch that headed back to dockside. On the way I looked around me. The smile on everyone's face told it all. There would be enough treasure tales to be yarned ashore for years to come.

Bob Weller, Mel Fisher, Pat Patterson celebrating the "Sueco" *silver recovery.*

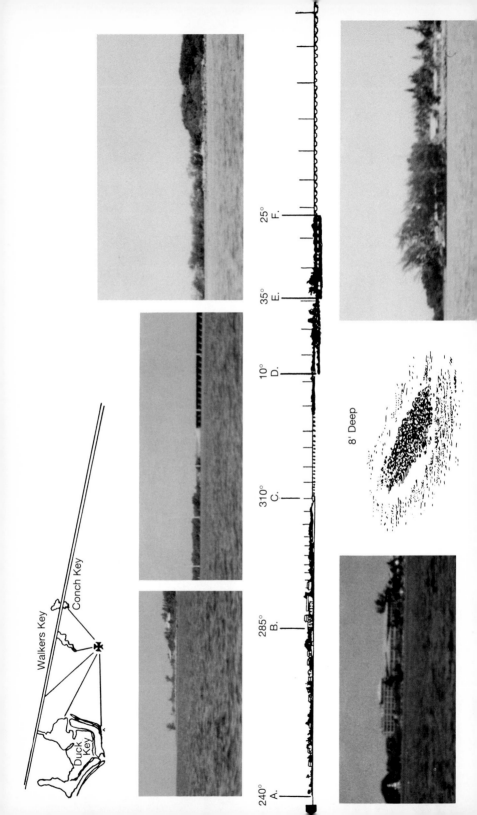

Walkers Key

Conch Key

Duck Key

240°
A.

285°
B.

310°
C.

10°
D.

35°
E.

25°
F.

8' Deep

Two guests from Honeywell and the author with his 16' salvage boat "Frogfoot."

The "Royal Fifth" group Brad Patten, Bob Weller, Ray Manier, Pat Patterson

The author in the stern of the "Big Fisherman" with conglomerates of silver coins and bar shot. Photo Credit: Pat Patterson.

The author with a handful of silver "Pieces of Eight" — Sueco

Intact olive jar — Sueco. *Photo Credit: E. Richards.*

Conglomerate of silver "Pieces of Eight" attached to a large iron spike. Note shard of porcelain Kang Hsi. *Photo Credit: Bob Weller.*

"Pillar Dollar"
From the 1733 Fleet. Photo Credits: E. Richards

Selected References

EL POPULO

WELLER, Robert "Frogfoot." "El Populo, 1733-1966," PLUS ULTRA Newsletter, 1st Quarter 1988.

H.M.S. WINCHESTER

BROOKFIELD, Charles M. "Cannon on Florida Reefs Solve Mystery of Sunken Ship," NATIONAL GEOGRAPHIC Magazine, December 1941.

COLLEDGE, J. J. "Ships of the Royal Navy - Volume I." Greenhill Books, London, 1969.

PETERSON, Mendel L. "History of Seafaring" - edited by George Bass, Chapter 11, 'Traders and Privateers Across the Atlantic: 1492-1733.' Walker. New York. 1972.

Royal Navy Files. Public Record Office, Kew, Richmond, Surrey, England TW9 4DU.
    A. ADM 52/120 Master's Log, H.M.S. Winchester, 11 April - 24 September, 1695.
    B. ADM 51/4395 Captain's Log, H.M.S. Winchester, 11 April - 20 September, 1695.
    C. ADM 1/5256-8 Court-Martial Enquiry, loss of H.M.S. Winchester. 1680.

WELLER, Robert "Frogfoot." "H.M.S. Winchester-1695," PLUS ULTRA Newsletter, 4th Quarter 1987.

SAN JOSÉ

WELLER, Robert "Frogfoot." "San Jose, 1728-1733," PLUS ULTRA Newsletter, 2nd Quarter 1989.

U.S.S. ALLIGATOR

CHAPELLE, H. I. "The History of American Sailing Ships." New York, 1935.

CHAPELLE, H.I. Plan of the U.S.S. Alligator. Naval Historical Center, Washington Navy Yard, Washington, D.C. 20374.

WELLER, Robert "Frogfoot." "The Buccaneers and the Alligator," PLUS ULTRA Newsletter, 3rd Quarter 1986.

ANGUSTIAS

WELLER, Robert Frogfoot". "Nuestra Senora de las Angustias," PLUS ULTRA Newsletter, 1st Quarter 1984.

WELLER, Robert. "Shipwreck Poem Leads to Sunken Treasure," SKIN DIVER Magazine, October 1974.

DE TOCA VELASCO, Don Jose Ignacio. "Triaca Producida de un Veneno." Madrid, 1734.

SUECO DE ARIZÓN

MEYLACH, Martin. "Diving to a Flash of Gold." Doubleday. Garden City, NY. 1971.

WELLER, Robert "Frogfoot." "The Sueco Silver," PLUS ULTRA Newsletter, 1st Quarter 1990.

1733 SPANISH PLATE FLEET - GENERAL

CONTRATACION 2003. Archivo de las Indias. Seville, Spain.

ESCRIBANIA DE CAMARA 1123A. Archivo de las Indias. Seville, Spain.

INDIFERENTE GENERAL 754. Dated September 6, 1734. Archivo General de las Indias.

Index